Recruitment Gems Uncovered

The Ultimate Guide to Guaranteed
Success & Wealth in Your Industry

Deenita Pattni

| Acknowledgements |

Throughout my journey to where I am now, there are a number of people who have impacted my life, the choices I have made and helped me get to where I am. They also helped me create this book. I'd like to take the time to acknowledge them...

Thanks to **Davin** and **Dipesh**. As my brothers, you have been two solid rocks in my life and, although we are all opinionated, I know those opinions have shaped me. Davin, thanks for using your amazing, visual mind to create my book cover. Dips, thanks for all your advice around marketing. Thanks to both of you for giving me the courage and confidence to believe I can do what I want and be successful in my entrepreneurial journey. Thanks also for the love and fun we have together. Love you both!

I've already mentioned my parents who are my life pillars. Thanks for the freedom and motivation you have both given me; **Dad**, your willpower continues to transform and inspire me. **Mum**, your unconditional support, love and kindness know no bounds. Love you both!

Thanks to my **whole extended family** – so many to mention – because you enrich my life for all the right reasons and I am filled with gratitude that I was born into this extended family.

I'd like to give my appreciation to those who have impacted my professional journey, which resulted in me not only writing this book, but also helped me be the best in the recruitment industry (especially when I was close to giving up). To my ex-boss and close friend, **Mike Berry**, thank you for continuing to support me in my entrepreneurial journey.

Thank you **Mike Quinn** and **Paul Farrer** for giving me an impactful introduction into recruitment. **Vix** and **Alan Binnie, Fred Knipe, Nick O'Connor**, thanks for your support in helping me continue in the industry and fall in love with it even more. To **Mike Fletcher, Emma Castle, Lesley May, Neil Hamilton**, my friends inside and outside work. Thanks also to **Jack Gratton**, Chairman of Major Players Recruitment and Andrew Rutherford, owner of MRA; as I started my journey as a business owner, you proved how industry colleagues, despite being in the same sector, could support each other in business.

A special mention to my amazing friend, sister, and constant support, my 'bestie': **Minal Thakarar**. You are an immediate source of inspiration, encouragement, and laughter and a reminder that life is there to be enjoyed and embraced.

You always need a mentor who is willing to stretch you to heights you never thought you could reach. For me, this person is undoubtedly **Andy Harrington**. Through his mentorship, training and friendship, my perspective, purpose and passion has evolved to a level that shows me my potential is limitless. He continues to be part of this journey and, in my eyes, a close friend forever.

A special heartfelt thanks goes to a lady who was instrumental in me completing my book and, even though I only met her in 2012, became a key source of inspiration. We laughed, cried and evolved together and her action-taking, all-or-nothing attitude was a catalyst in me taking more action in my own life! There is a reason some people enter your life – and there are 1000+ reasons why **Cheryl Chapman** did. I am grateful for that.

Thanks to **Tosin Ogunnusi**, the man who sold me a promise of unlimited opportunity in 2004 and connected me with people who delivered on that promise. Tosin, you became a genuine friend, who gives from the heart and an older brother with whom I enjoy my debates!

My fellow original **ACE Mentors** with whom I began the journey, who became my support in helping me build my business: **Ruth, Miles, Sammy, Andrea, Marion, Simon, Sanjeev** and subsequently all the ACE Team who came after and have become lifelong friends.

Thanks to my good friend **Simon Coulson** who has always shared his advice freely and presented me with opportunities to speak on his platform. Thanks also to **Shaa Wasmund MBE**, who showed me how to be a strong woman in business without losing the female perspective and offered her support from a place of unconditional giving. Thanks also to my guest writers who dedicated their time to contribute to my book: **Sammy Blindell, Miles Fryer** (also my ex-roomie) and **Jo Smallbones.**

Thanks to **Raymond Aaron, Lori Murphy, Vishal Morjaria, Dyann Olivieira** and the rest of the 10-10-10 team for convincing me I had a book inside of me and supporting me along the way. Thanks to **Tim Kenning** for the illustrations and **Joe Gregory** for the key introductions.

To all my friends, mentors, mentees, crew and experts who have played a part in my personal and professional development journey from **Fire Your Desire, Inner Compass and Power to Achieve.** Too many names to mention but you know who you are – your support is priceless. A special mention to the team at Jet Set Speaker – your support & friendship really is priceless and precious.

The final mention is for absent friends and family: **Peter Fry** who really did present me with a path that I am extremely grateful for. You who left this universe way too early but will forever be in my heart of how to live and love life and everything I do. **My Nan and Granddad** whom I loved dearly and had a close bond with throughout the early part of my life. Nani, I know you've sent a message in your own way to let me know that embarking on my entrepreneurial journey was what I was born to do. With this faith, I stay committed and encouraged. Love you and miss both of you very much. And my uncle Vinu – who left this world prematurely and with it a huge void. You will always bring a smile to my face as I remember the 'joker' in you. My life changed forever the moment you left for heaven. Love you always.

| Foreword |

I first met Deenita Pattni in 2012 whilst speaking in London during a business seminar. What was immediately apparent was her passion to serve others and help them become a better version of themselves. It didn't take me long to realize that this approach existed within her DNA. She had a willingness to help, a strong approach to selling, an understanding of psychology and mindset transformation and a commitment and dedication to getting results. Her charisma both on and off stage is authentic and inspiring, making you want to immediately connect with and learn from her.

Recruitment Gems Uncovered is written by someone who undoubtedly knows the industry inside and out and isn't afraid to challenge its myths and unfair reputation. This book is more than the information that is in it. It's a Bible that adds a new dimension to techniques and tools used in recruitment training.

Having entered the industry in 1999 and almost given up after 3 months, it doesn't surprise me that Deenita sought alternative ways to improve her skills and overcome the challenges of working in a competitive, sales environment. Knowing that there are many other recruiters out there who continue to experience the same challenges, Deenita has put her knowledge and knowhow into a powerful system for one simple reason: to help others. She aims to help talented recruiters master the techniques, reach their goals, make a profit and remain in the industry.

Considering the recruitment industry is one which requires quick thinking, a multi-tasking approach, an adaptable attitude, business acumen and clear, engaging communication skills, I can't think of anyone better suited to teach the methodologies of successful recruiting than Deenita herself. Having experienced these traits first-hand, she would easily and effectively make an impactful contribution to the performance of a sales-led business.

| **Foreword** | continued

Recruitment can be a tough, unpredictable, pressurized and thankless industry to work in and too many potentially great recruiters depart prematurely due to the lack of empowered training. This book changes that. It will show you the key elements to master to become an outstanding performer in recruitment regardless of your background or experience before you entered. Broken down into small chunks and explained with purpose and practical examples, it promises to be a reference book you keep on your desk at all times.

If you want to be a true success in recruitment, deal with people in an authentic and caring way, and make money at the same time (without selling your soul), then this book shows you exactly how you can be a respected, trustworthy and go-to-expert that candidates and clients will **rely** on, **recommend** to others and **remain** with.

It's been my pleasure to write this foreword for Deenita Pattni. As a New York Times Best Selling Author, I'm happy to associate my name with hers.

Raymond Aaron
New York Times' Best Selling Author

| Contents |

| **Preface** |

Recruitment is an industry that has been around for years and it's not disappearing any time soon. Some of you may read that statement and be ready to argue it. And I know why. You see, it's not disappearing; after all, the recruitment industry is one of the fastest-growing industries globally. And it's also one that is changing – constantly. If you want to remain at the top of the game and be the recruitment professional of choice, there are a few incentives you must adopt:

| **Incentive 1** | Overcome your fears.

When you enter the world of recruitment, the role itself is one that exposes you – both good and bad. You're discovered for everything you are brilliant at and exposed for all parts of you that aren't...yet! And these parts of you are simply FEARS: fears of rejection, being wrong, the unknown, failure, being judged. I believe fears are there for you to overcome; as Susan Jeffers' famously titled book, 'Face the Fear and Do It Anyway.' Your recruitment career will soar.

| **Incentive 2** | Selling is serving!

The recruitment industry is not just for people who like selling. And if you're reading this and believe that, you're wrong. People who enter the industry do so because they want to help and serve others. So, if you've always wanted a career that changes people's lives, where you make a difference, where you help someone follow their dreams, recruitment is perfect.

| **Incentive 3** | In it for the long-term!

Whether you're recruiting candidates into permanent jobs or interim, temp roles, you must think long-term. Too many recruiters see their clients and candidates as short-term stock trades and drop them if their stock price isn't high enough or when a better investment comes along. To be seen as a game-changer, as someone who challenges the (unnecessary) reputation the industry has gained, you need to see your 'commodity' instead as real people and long-term prospects.

| **Incentive 4** | It's all about communication!

Whether you call it recruitment, career counseling, matching jobs to people – what we are in the business of amounts to one key thing. We are in the business of COMMUNICATION. Whether it's to clients, candidates, clients to candidates, peer to peer – as a recruiter, that's what we are in the business of. Perfecting this skill in the right way is key. How you communicate can make the difference between making money and not. A presupposition taught in NLP created by Richard Bandler and John Grinder state 'The Meaning of Communication is the Response YOU get!' Guess what? If the response isn't what you hoped for – change your communication. Your results will transform.

| **Incentive 5** | Make a stop at the service station.

The recruitment industry travels in the fast lane. New technology and platforms are consistently emerging, making recruitment more efficient and cost-effective for employers. Embrace it, stay ahead of it and excel. But don't forget that our commodity is people and somewhere along this journey you need to step out of the car and ensure face-to-face contact.

| **Incentive 6** | Value yourself.

With competitors at your heels, it's so easy to give in to ridiculous fees. What you do as a recruiter, often on a contingency basis (where money comes in only when you've delivered the goods), is priceless. The time taken to source, interview, and bring to the forefront the best talent for a business is valuable. Believe in the fact that you're providing a premier service and ensure the price reflects that. And do not let anyone tell you otherwise. As long as you deliver on what you promise, you are worth every penny and more for the role you play at the price you charge.

| **Incentive 7** | You are a BRAND.

Regardless of the brand you work for, be very clear on this next point. You are a BRAND in and of yourself. Candidates and clients will work with the company you are employed by because of the service YOU deliver. So, as a brand, you have got to stand for something. What is it? What's the reason you do what you do?

What type of recruiter do you want to be known as and remembered for? Whatever it is for you – LIVE IT, BREATHE IT AND SHOW IT.

| **Incentive 8** | There is no FAILURE, only FEEDBACK.

There is one thing you are guaranteed when you work in recruitment. Not every deal will go your way. People will change their minds at the last hurdle; they'll call you in the final hour to tell you they aren't coming. They'll reject an offer and stay where they are and a whole host of other reasons you'll come across in your lifetime. You've got to take each and every moment like that and learn from it. Evaluate your performance. Even if there is nothing you could have done, there will be a new insight to walk away with

| **Incentive 9** | Your GOALS are ONE.

Competition is essential in this industry and when you're competing with your colleagues to get high on that leaderboard it's fun and incentivising. However, don't allow competition to get the better of you. That's how conflict begins internally and soon you forget that you're all in the same company for the same reason: to be the best and make money whilst you're at it. Instead let the competition drive you as a team so that as individuals you all benefit. Even if you're always striving to be number one on that league table, ensure you carry the team with you so you make it to the top as a company and also keep your people with you until the end.

| **Incentive 10** | Be yourself!

Be hungry, be motivated and have the desire. Also, be your genuine true self. People buy into people. As Zig Ziglar said, *"they'll do business with you when they both LIKE and TRUST you."* To succeed in recruitment, you need not be an aggressive, money-grabbing, sell-your-soul-to-the-devil recruiter. Stay genuine, stay authentic and ensure integrity in everything you do. You'll survive in the industry for a lot longer, for all the right reasons and have clients asking for you by name.

'If you do what you've always done, you'll get what you've always gotten'

MARK TWAIN

| **Prologue** |

It's been six months since I returned back to England.

Another letter: as I open it up, I can hear my heart pounding. What will this one say? Will it be the same as the 198 I have previously opened?

"Dear Deenita...It was lovely to meet you last week and get to know more about you."

I'm used to that beginning – same as the others. Although I feel this has a slightly different ring to it. I smile as I skim to the third paragraph.

"Unfortunately..." I don't need to read on. I know it already. The beginning of that sentence is so familiar – same as the others. As I glance up, with the smile well and truly gone, my friend Vimal looks at me. "Don't worry, Dee, it's not the end of the world. Something will come up."

Vimal, my friend since childhood, with her warm caring big brown eyes, smiled her gigantic, soothing smile at me. She always had a way of seeing a different perspective when it came to her friends.

"In fact, Dee, I was scouring the paper for jobs the other day and there seem to be lots of jobs in recruitment. The role involves working with people, which you are really good at – you should give it a go!"

"I understand, Vimal, but it would mean doing something else instead of what I have always wanted to do, since I was a child."

"Dee, I'm not saying give up on it. You just need to look at other options when things aren't working, and get out there again. Do it for a little while until you find your dream job, then leave. Nothing has to be forever."

Me with Vimal

She had a point. I needed to get out of the house, meet new people and get my confidence back. The 199 letters had started to take their toll on me.

Little did I know how a change in direction would result.

CHAPTER 1
WHERE IT ALL BEGAN

| **Chapter 1** - Where it All Began |

I've been in the recruitment industry for more than 15 years. And it'd be fair to say that, to last that long in recruitment, you definitely need a thick skin. But maybe for you, like me, it wasn't something you were born with...

If you'd been with me, back in November of 1999, you would have been sat at my desk in a busy, buzzy office working for one of London's major media recruiters for a couple of months. It was the best seat in the office. Facing the window, where every now and again, you'd see the London Eye being constructed ready for the millennium. My desk was a charcoal grey with blue dividers separating me from my teammates.

My manager, Tim, walked in, with his usual pin stripe suit, shiny black shoes and interesting choice in ties. He was a colourful character – a bit like Gordon Brittas from Brittas Empire. **"Welcome team,"** he bellowed. *"It's 5 past 9 – lets hit those phones and make some calls."* I was given the clients from letters D to G to call.

Every call I made, my mouth was dry, and my hands were sweaty. I prepared for the worst. *"Good morning. May I speak to David Spencer please?"* *"Sorry, we don't use agencies!"* *"Don't call us, we'll call you!"* *"Haven't got time to talk to you!"* *"Not interested!"* *"Sorry, we have a PSL. Not interested."*

85% of the time, these were the responses to my calls. Sound familiar?

I'd been making new business calls for the last two months; it wasn't easy and I didn't like it.
I was always wondering when the real job of helping people find jobs was going to start.

Until Tim revealed to me one struggling afternoon: *"Dee! This is recruitment."*

What!?! I thought it was all about helping people out there get their dream jobs. I was two months into my probation period and all I'd done was constantly pick up the phone and sell to people I didn't know and get them to give me business. I'm not a salesperson!

Ever remember feeling that way? Perhaps you still feel like that sometimes?

www.viamii.com/training

I had people hang up on me, gatekeepers recognise my voice and tell me not to call back and clients tell me that they weren't interested. I constantly felt I was wasting their time when I called, disturbing them. I felt like a door-to-door double-glazing salesperson forcing people to listen to me sell them something they don't want. I felt everyone in the office looking at me, which made me even more nervous.

I was so happy when Friday arrived, not because the weekend had come but because the week had ended. I couldn't even remember the good calls because I just focused on the bad.

One day, I'd reached my threshold. The pressure was on and I could feel it. I was ready to pack it in. This wasn't worth it; I'd made a decision: tomorrow would be my last day.

Do you have someone in your life that inspires you? For me, there was one person. As I contemplated giving up, it took me back to his story.

If you'd been with me back in 1988, you would have been in front of a true gentleman, a family man. KP was his name and he was always the life of the party. He had looked after his mother since the age of 13 and brought up his three younger siblings. He was a real risk taker. Having worked for other people all his life, every now and again, he'd try his hand at running his own business, only to find it didn't work. But each time he fell, he got right back up.
He had a glass half-full attitude to life. Loved to dance, sing and was a real performer of life. Great things always come in small packages. And, at 5'4", he most definitely was great.

And then one day, he had another fall – only this time it was different…

You would have been standing next to me in the grey, disinfectant-doused environment. I remember the doctor speaking to my Mum. *"Mr. Pattni has contracted a condition called Guillain–Barré syndrome. It's a rare tropical disease and has damaged his nerves. It's unlikely he will ever walk again."* Those were the last words I remember before I heard my mum crying.

After a month in hospital, we took him home in a wheelchair. My mum had to feed, bathe and dress him as he had lost sensation in his arms and legs – and he wasn't happy about it! He felt he had lost his status…his place…. his position! But somewhere from inside he had kept hold of a part of him that defined who he was; he still kept hold of determination, willpower, and belief.

'Many of life's failures are people who did not realize how close they were to success when they gave up'

THOMAS EDISON

He put in months of physical exercise, hours of perseverance, and minutes of pain as he rehabilitated himself, at a time when the medical profession had given up hope. My Dad, KP, exhausted and tired, where others would have said *"no more,"* instead strived for more!

Within 18 months, my Dad had beaten the odds: he had taken his first steps and started walking again. Within two years he started a business from home and restored within him the man he always was....

My willpower...my Dad!
It doesn't matter how many times you fall, only how many times you get up.
He taught me that!

That night, 24 hours before I was going to say "no more" and give up, I decided instead to strive for more. I went back the next day not ready to resign, but determined to beat the odds.

Within the first couple of years, I produced good results in recruitment. I continued to learn ways and methods to make the recruitment process better. I was trained in numerous sales techniques and was always willing to invest in my growth, sometimes learning the same things over and over again.

Although I was doing well, my wins were inconsistent and my losses consistent. I knew I had to change something to increase the wins and turn the losses around, but had no idea what.

What was still missing?

Every time I faced failure, my inner talk emerged. Whatever I said to myself just made me feel deflated, demotivated, and dejected. And every time this happened, it left an ounce more of self-doubt behind, which took ages to overcome. All the training helped me in the short-term but, after a while, I was stuck and needing a way forward.

A weekend in November of 2004 revealed this missing part to me. If you'd been with me, you would have been sat next to me at a seminar in London run by a gentleman called Andy Harrington. As he took to the stage, his small, petite build was a far cry from the presence he exuded on stage! The event looked into the human psyche and the things that held us back from success and what was required to overcome them.

In a hotel room sat with 300 other people, I only focused on Andy, as he owned the stage and every word he shared with the audience. One sentence stood out for me from the whole weekend. Andy looked me right in the eye as he stood there and said:

"Fail your way to Success."

Did you know that 85% of us allow fear to out-do our success?

Andy Harrington had failed his way to success.

Here's the thing, though. The recruitment industry doesn't always allow for failures. Could that be the very reason that it stops us from reaching our true success

Everything I learned that weekend was the foundation of NLP (Neuro-Linguistic Programming – more about this further along in the book).

You may even recognise it by another name: Jedi mind tricks or Yoda wisdom. Whatever label you put on it, it doesn't change its powerful effect. In its simplest form, it's the study of how you communicate more effectively. Not just with other people – which is a great trait to have in recruitment – but also with yourself, which is a must-have attribute in recruitment. And that is exactly the piece that was missing.

I read somewhere that what you think about, you bring about. And that's what I'd been doing. It was time to start thinking differently.

My results transformed... My placement ratio got better, my influence over candidates improved. I turned *"no's"* into *"yeses."* On days where things didn't go my way (and let's face it, we do have those days), I stopped asking myself *"why"* and instead asked *"how?" "How can I stop it from happening again?"* As a result, I became a top-ranking biller in every company where I worked.

My colleagues saw the results I got and wanted the same. I shared the tools and techniques I share with many today so they could discover that raw talent, the gems buried deep within them.

And that's why I love sharing these gems with professionals like you. I see and know of too many recruiters who either gave up on themselves or weren't given a chance because, like me, the crucial piece was missing that would have led to their success. They just didn't realise that piece was within them.

| The Liberator |

Back in 1942, there was a diamond prospector who decided to try his luck on a dry riverbed in his native land. Like many others in his land, Solano was poor and his luck had run out. For weeks and months, Solano would dig deeper in the dirt and pick out pebbles from the hundreds of stones – only to find a plain rock. Dejected, demotivated and deflated, he decided he had had enough. He was ready to give up and go home. He would say he tried it and gave it his all – but it wasn't meant to be.

Before he did, he decided to give it one more desperate go! He drew his hand out and as he opened it, he saw a sand encrusted stone. He measured, weighed it and it was indeed a diamond.

Harry Winston, a diamond dealer in New York, paid Solano a handsome sum. The diamond today is known as *"The Liberator"* and is considered one of the purest and largest in the world.

I have a real passion and admiration for people who choose to work in recruitment and that's why, unlike many, I stayed in the profession so that I could help others. Today, years later, I'm so glad I get to help recruiters dig that little bit deeper and uncover that gem that's always been within them.

Diamonds are made out of the carbon that explodes due to the pressure from stars! It's the same carbon we're made out of.

For many recruiters, you're sitting on a piece of land with gems undiscovered. It's time to uncover long-lasting, hidden talent that is present within our industry. It is present within you.

You're all capable of reaching your goals in recruitment; whether you're new to the industry or you've been around the block a few times, whether you come from a sales or recruitment background or something unrelated. If you want a profession where you not only piece together the futures of others, but craft yourself a future that gives you both reward and richness, then you're in the right place.

Recruitment Gems - Uncovered will share many of the techniques I used throughout my career that made me great money, brought me immense success with genuine integrity and an ethical approach. Use these enough times, and you too will enjoy great results and a rewarding, rapid-result career that you'll want to be part of for a long time.

My mentor Andy Harrington who taught me to overcome my limiting beliefs and with whom I continue my personal development journey through so that I can help professionals in the industry achieve success.

'The definition of Insanity is doing the same thing over and over again and expecting a different result'.

ALBERT EINSTEIN

CHAPTER 2
THE RECRUITMENT INDUSTRY & **YOU**

———————

| **Chapter 2 -** The Recruitment Industry & YOU |

Let me begin by asking two questions: Are you motivated by success? And would you like to experience success more often and make more money as a result?

I would imagine, if you're a recruiter reading this, you have answered YES to both of the above.

Perhaps today, you're a recruiter who's struggling in a competitive environment; you may have once been at the top of your game but today are finding it hard to reach your target. Maybe you're new to the industry and feel you've been thrown into the deep end. It just seems too hard for you; you feel you're in too deep. Possibly you're starting to lose your best clients to your competitors or your almost-deals are falling at the last hurdle. Potentially you or your team just isn't performing and the pressure is on. As a manager, you're no longer leading by example and you're losing respect from those you manage. As a result, you're working longer hours, fighting for the attention of your clients and candidates and starting to feel burned out. You might be wondering whether recruitment is for you. You're beginning to lose your confidence as you compare yourself to others or to yourself and your past results.

Instead, imagine a different picture where you are at the top of that leader board, not once, not twice, but all the time. Your role still inspires you and gets you out of bed in the morning with a spring in your step called success. Your success is contagious and, as a result, your team or peers around you want to follow you; they see you as someone to model. As a recruiter, you're admired not just by people you work with, but also by others in the industry. Your competitors know who you are and hate coming against you. You're respected in the industry, always evolving and developing. Your clients come to you because they know you're the best. For candidates and clients, YOU are the recruiter of choice.

So let me ask you this: to get from where you are currently (a place of uncertainty and doubt), to where you'd like to be (back to being passionate and successful about the industry you work in), would you agree that you need to adopt new strategies from the ones you've been using? Absolutely, because as the infamous Craig Valentine once said, *"what got you here, won't get you there."* Meaning, in order to continue success, you need to continuously change and invest in your development. When something isn't working, change it and do something new.

You see, in any industry, personal development is key. And I believe that investing in your own personal development in recruitment is paramount to your success. And here's why:

Research carried out in 2014 showed that despite recruiters being in a profession that finds people for companies and jobs for people, recruitment businesses themselves actually have the highest staff turnover. Bit of a conflict there, don't you think? How can we be so brilliant at finding other businesses the right people, yet unable to nurture talent within our own businesses?

The reason? Not enough time is invested in personally developing staff. You need it and want it, but at the same time you're needed at your desk. You're required to be striking deals and bringing in the cash. This works when the market is on your side, when the economy is on the up and clients are knocking on your door, but that's not always the case. When the market turns, competitors appear and business isn't so forthcoming; as a recruiter, you can be left unprepared and untrained.

And when performance levels fall, potentially great recruiters are seen as the problem, only replacing them becomes harder. Why? Because recruitment businesses are either holding onto their best people or too many good ones have left the industry simply because someone didn't take the time to develop them into the successful recruiter they were destined to be.

Is this you?

That's what really provides the foundation for this book. As you go through the chapters, you will pick up advice, tips and information that will help you reach new heights in your recruitment career. They may be strategies that you have either forgotten about due to complacency or ones you have never tried, used, or come across.

Whether you're a recruiter who's picked this book up or a manager or owner of a recruitment business, the message is the same. Personal development and training are paramount in the recruitment industry. If you're someone who wants to stay ahead of the curve, be the best in your industry, challenge the status quo and be seen as the recruiter of choice by both clients and candidates, then the chapters in the book will give you the groundwork you need to reach the heights of success.

Because here's the real truth: the industry is moving at lightning speed and it shows no sign of slowing down. Competition is on the rise and I don't just mean other agency businesses. Technology, social media, new recruitment platforms, LinkedIn and more innovative avenues are showing up and giving the market alternative methods. But here's what I believe and hope you do too: Recruiters are still very much a force to be reckoned with; our industry continues to grow both in terms of people and revenue and we most certainly do provide a service that mirrors no other, one that *'pieces together futures.'*

You need to be an action-taker when it comes to your own career; by investing in your own personal development you too can "piece together YOUR future" within this industry.

The choice is yours!

'TRAINING ISN'T JUST FOR CHRISTMAS, BUT FOR LIFE'.

DEENITA PATTNI

CHAPTER 3
THE 5 GEMS
UNCOVERED

| **Chapter 3 -** The 5 Gems Uncovered |

Throughout my years working in recruitment and personal development, I've discovered there are five fundamental areas you need to truly master to become great at recruitment. "Only five?" I hear you say. Yes, only five, but once you grasp these five, you ultimately become the recruiter of choice in a highly competitive industry.

These five specific areas working in tandem with each other is what will separate you from your competition, differentiate the great from the good and raise your profile in the industry.

You see, the recruitment landscape has changed and continues to change at an accelerating pace. And as the industry moves on at this rapid pace, in order to stay in the game, many recruiters get left behind. Why?

Simple. Training and development has been a low priority; either the training world hasn't always kept up and so their techniques are too "old school" or training has been considered a nice-to-have instead of a must-have.

We're now in the information age and, as recruitment professionals and experts in developing the careers of others, we also need to be developed. The five modules (which I cover in depth on my live Rapid Recruitment Programme and will uncover in this book) will not only help you as a recruiter perform at your peak today, but will also give you the tools to perform at your peak moving forward no matter what the market challenge!

So, let's take a look at these five key areas:

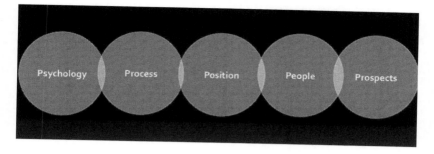

The first area you need to master

Psychology: There's a great quote by Henry Ford who says, "Whether you think you can or you think you can't, you're right" and this could not be more appropriate when it comes to the recruitment profession. And I, for one, am definitely evidence of this quote and how the shift in my mindset changed me from being an "I can't" person to an "I can" person. Recruitment ultimately falls under the sales category. That's what we do. We sell! We sell our service to clients, sell jobs to candidates and sell candidates to clients. We continue to sell propositions to each of these parties from the start of the process right through to the end and thereafter. Yet the word "sales" is what scares people, especially if you're a recruiter who has come into the profession from the industry you're now recruiting within.

Sales is simply the ability to influence. But why is it that some recruiters can influence clients with, in essence, the exact same proposition and succeed whilst others fail? How do some recruiters continue to increase their Net Fee Income when others find it challenging to meet targets? How specifically do recruiters still hit big in an economic downturn when others choose to leave the profession due to how tough it becomes? It all boils down to mindset and not only how we communicate with others (clients, candidates, teams), but also (more importantly) how we communicate with ourselves.

The truth is, every economy goes through a cycle and every successful recruiter has worked through that by adopting a mindset that helps him or her to change perspective and be flexible enough to see where the opportunity exists instead. The ability to do that lives within the recruiter; he or she simply asks better quality questions internally and therefore receives better quality answers. The mission is big enough for the recruiter to resist seeing the problem and instead see the opening.

Opportunities are in front of us, around us and to the side of us every single day, sometimes even staring us in the face. However, if your inner dialogue continues to tell you they don't exist, like with anything in life, you'll soon start to believe it. And your actions will follow.

You've no doubt heard someone say or maybe even told yourself, "It's a lot simpler than it looks." That is true of many things in life. However, the way we're shaped and moulded comes from our beliefs, life experiences, values, upbringing, etc. So, when a situation occurs, we give a meaning to it that has been complicated by the beliefs we hold to be true. But what if those beliefs no longer hold true? What if those very beliefs are holding us back? Stopping us from doing the things we can? Stopping us from being successful?

I remember when I first started in recruitment, 85% of my role was cold-calling. Yes – that's what they called it in those days. When I got a "no", a telephone receiver slammed down on me, a "go away, we hate recruiters" response, I took it personally. I told myself I wasn't good enough, I was wrong and they were right, I was disturbing them, I shouldn't be pestering them, I'm no good at this. I shouldn't, I must not, I am not, I can't, I won't…

'Whether you think you can or you think you can't, you're right'

HENRY FORD

What I continued to tell myself only knocked my confidence whilst at the same time gave me the excuse I needed to console myself. Did I learn anything from it? Could I see another way? No! I was too blinded by everything that had gone wrong to see how I could turn things around. What if, instead, I simply asked "how?" How could I phrase my opening better? How could I improve my sales? How could I get past the gatekeeper? How could grab his attention in a different way? For what purpose did the client respond in that way? How could I understand his position better and what specifically is the objection? Would that inner dialogue have gotten me different results? Absolutely! And they did, a few years later, once I mastered the techniques that helped me shift my mindset to one that was more empowering. Do I still have bad deals and lose out on business? Of course…it's part and parcel of working with people. But I question, learn, adapt and take accountability for changing the things I can and need to change.

This perspective eliminates the self-destructive talk and moves me on faster.

Only when you start to focus on what's possible and focus on the solution do your problems become insignificant in comparison. If there's a problem, there must exist a solution because you wouldn't recognise one without the other. As recruitment professionals, you fall into one of two categories (as positioned by Eldridge Cleaver) "You're either part of the problem, or you're part of the solution" – which one are you?

All successful recruiters adopt the right psychology – whether they know it or not. Do this and you start to see every other element of the recruitment process in a different way. Imagine coming across any challenge and not just being able to overcome it but moving on from it.

Now let's just be clear! That doesn't mean you won't come across some of the usual pitfalls recruitment throws out; placements may still be turned down, candidates may still back out last minute, and clients may still decide to say "no." But how you respond and bounce back will be transformed when you apply the right mindset! What you say to yourself and do next will lead you to a place of continued success, drive and motivation. And, of course, revenue!

The second area you need to master to be an outstanding and successful recruiter is the **process**. To be a successful recruiter you have to know how to recruit (obviously). You need to know where to start, the 'how to' of the industry. You need to know the sequence and steps that take you from the beginning to the end. This isn't any different from most training programmes out there except for one thing. You've mastered the art of step one, the art of managing your psychology, the art of applying a winner's mindset so now when you learn everything in this step, you do so with a winner's perspective, a winner's state of mind. You learn how to make a sales call, influence others, interview candidates, probe, generate leads, handle objections, and manage your time effectively. Doing all of these techniques from a place of fear ultimately stops you from reaching top gear; here you grasp them with the right mindset.

Influence is an interesting concept. The process of recruitment is more than just selling and making placements. In recruitment, people are our commodity whether they come in the form of a candidate or client. So, our primary role is to influence them to take us up on our service, to consider a role, to consider a job offer or to consider our candidate above someone else.

So, how do we do that? How do we influence another person whether by phone or face-to-face to consider a different perspective? One simple yet impactful step – this is done through the art of communication. One key aspect in making all areas within the recruitment process work is the way we communicate with others. People use different modes of language to interpret information and connect. Speaking in a different mode to the one your client or candidate can understand, is the same as speaking French to someone who only understands English. So, if someone is more visual and they tend to communicate and comprehend with pictures, then use visually descriptive words and phrases such as, "I can see that" or, "I can picture that." So the more powerful way to influence this person is to converse with them using their mode of communication. There are 4 different modes: visual, auditory, kinesthetic and auditory digital. Once you master the different words and phrases and recognise what your client or candidate's primary mode is, you will be able to match them, giving you more sway over them by speaking to them in their language. Once you master this, selling, interviewing, and persuading will all become easier, helping you to achieve better placement ratios than your competition.

Once you have mastered your psychology and key aspects of the recruitment process itself, one area that many training courses don't cover comes third. That is the **position.**

In this business, people buy people. We've heard this time and time again; clients invest time working with you once they know, like, and trust you. What this means is you need to ensure that right from the get-go, you position yourself as the recruiter of choice. Whether it be organically, in a networking environment or when you're presenting in front of a client, you want to make sure you're the one who is at the forefront of everyone's mind. Recruiters crumble at the thought of standing up in front of people where they will be asked questions and assessed on their service. Winning people over is a must and it's part and parcel of your role.

And it's not just you. At the same time, as an ambassador for the agency you work for, you also need to understand the best way to position your **organisation**, whether that be networking at industry events, during a pitch presentation, or online.

There is etiquette to how you do this; as quickly as your reputation and position can rise to the top, it can also be damaged if not done right.

So, when positioning yourself, if you're failing to get yourself known, if nobody really knows what you do and WHY you do it, if clients and candidates aren't able to recognize WHY your organisation is the one to opt for, then you fade into the sea of sameness. And let me tell you, the recruitment ocean is huge. Once you float into the distance, it's hard to swim back in front.

Next, let's look at the fourth element.

PEOPLE: As I mentioned before, people are our commodity. Like other commodities their price can fluctuate (salary) and they can make you money as well as lose you money with an unexpected change. But, unlike other commodities, they can speak back and have a conversation with you and you cannot always predict their reactions.
One of the fundamental flaws made by many recruiters, rookie or not, is their reluctance to interact with people.

The truth is: if you're in recruitment, your results rely on this taking place for many reasons.

First, you consistently need to be finding fresh talent. Once you've positioned yourself, candidates and clients who find you want to get to know you. There are a number of competitors you have and they're all after the same candidates – so you must ensure you get hold of them first.

Next, once you've found them, you need to get a better idea of what it is they want: what's their WHY? What do they really desire and what needs do they want met? When you understand this, selling jobs to them becomes an art form and gets you a YES every time! This understanding you gain around communicating with your clients and candidates means you can influence them better. When you sell a job to them, you don't just sell the mechanics of the job, you need to fire off the desires the candidates have about their next role.

And one thing to remember that is easily overlooked: Human interaction is not just external. A major flaw in recruiters reaching six figures is their inability to work as a team. Yes, you work in sales and you want to do what's best for you. However, what you'll find is when you start to work together better, your results increase both as an individual and as a business. You need to understand the bigger picture and learn the best way to deal with internal conflicts and politics before they become out of hand and end up blocking your results.

All of the above three have one thing in common: you have to communicate, whether on the phone or in person. None of the above would work hiding behind your computer screen.

Yes, online resources like LinkedIn, blogs and Twitter absolutely have a place in this digital age and are key tools for positioning yourself and consistently being visible. At the same time, they can become a hindrance. Technology has resulted in recruiters preferring to stay at their desks, communicate via email and stay hidden behind their email. If that's what you prefer, you're in the wrong business. Interacting with people LIVE has got to be your number one priority. Social media and technology has allowed us to advance and become efficient. Candidates, clients and information are more accessible to us and we are more accessible and visible to those who need us. But, whatever happens online must then be taken offline if you're to become a great recruiter.

This leads us to the final piece that all successful recruiters must master. This is crucial as a recruiter. And that is winning the right **prospects.**

Recruiters often have a "spray and pray" approach to their market when it comes to attracting prospects. In a desperate plea to meet targets, bring in jobs, and show they are working hard, they attempt to serve the whole market instead of segmenting or niching. 'Mapping' the market is key. When you map the market, you take a more in-depth look at what is out there, where the right opportunities are and how you can leverage them. You will discover an approach that does not have you wasting focus or time in exchange for little or no reward.

Trying to be all things to all people will keep you constantly chasing. By taking some time to plan your approach and assess the best areas will keep you motivated for longer and bring in successes quicker. Not to mention, it will ultimately build you a profitable portfolio of clients.

Successful recruiters map their markets the same way an athlete will map his route; an athlete will know exactly the route he needs to take in order to reach the next element of the triathlon. He will know how he needs to get there, what route will be the easiest and how much he needs to do to get there. Yes there is a whole lot around goals, visualisation and mindset he needs before all of that (hence why we cover this all first in the programme). But by mapping his route, he knows that this will give him the fastest completion time in return.

Recruitment Gems Uncovered is designed to take you through each of these areas and show you how you can master each of them to become the recruiter of choice. The following chapters will give you a perspective like no other on how recruitment can be the perfect career choice and how you can progress to lasting success, whether you're a novice, someone experienced, or someone who has chosen recruitment as their second career. Packed with expert advice, this is one industry bible you won't want to put down! Enjoy.

'Give a man a fish, you'll feed him for the day. Teach a man to fish and you feed him for a lifetime'.

CHINESE PROVERB

CHAPTER 4
THE RAPID RECRUITMENT ENGINE™

| **Chapter 4 -** The Rapid Recruitment Engine™ |

To help recruiters make six figure results, I teach them **The Rapid Recruitment Engine™**, which takes them through all elements of the recruitment cycle. Whether you're new to the game or experienced already, uncovering these five gems gives you all you need to become a key player in the industry and reach league-topping results.

To help my clients understand the recruiter's **PSYCHOLOGY,** they go through **The Mind Management Map™.** When training recruiters on my Rapid Recruitment Engine™, the psychology is one of the first things we cover. Why? Well, once you get this right, you have the opportunity to recognise just how amazing each opportunity is in recruitment. This module features the relevant NLP-based techniques that you can learn, understand and apply in your role as a recruiter.

That's exactly what gets uncovered in this module. We teach you how to overcome those negative thoughts and beliefs, how to get past those frustrating days in recruitment, how to best understand yourself and other people so that you can remain motivated and solution-focused for years to come (not just for the moment or for the few weeks that follow a training seminar). Your mindset focuses on success instead of failure and, as a result, you continue to develop and grow as a professional. When my clients complete my training, they walk out with tools that will keep them succeeding in the recruitment industry long-term!

To help my clients come to grips with each part of the recruitment **PROCESS** in detail, they learn **The Placement PROFIT Generator™.**

Here, you will learn six key strategies of the recruitment process. Recruiters who remain average do so because they either haven't been through these in as much detail as they should or, if they've gained any training in the past, they take the power of these strategies for granted. They focus on the end goal so much that they forget the intricacies of the steps needed to get to the goal in the first place.

What you learn in this framework are those small steps that get you to the right outcome quicker so you're seen as the recruiter of choice!

What you walk away with are strategies that you can mold and shape to whichever industry, role, and frequency you recruit for.

Look around and you'll find yourself surrounded by competitors in your industry. To help my clients **POSITION** themselves as true experts, they are taken through **The Rave and Refer Radar™.**

You learn three important techniques on how to become the recruiter everyone sees, remembers and calls upon when it comes to recruiting or finding their roles. You will no longer have to waste time hunting for the ideal candidate or client, as they will have already connected with you at some level and developed a basic level of trust.

What you will get from this framework is a way of building credibility, visibility and authority in your market place.

In order to help my clients really interact and get "buy in" with the one constant commodity, **PEOPLE,** we have the **The Effective Influencer™.**

You have to ask yourself, whether in business or personally, how much would you TRUST someone you hadn't met, someone you hadn't found out much about, or someone you didn't really know. So, why should relationships in recruitment be any different? Our personalities are different and there may well be some of you who are brilliant at interacting whereas others simply aren't sure how to be better at this. Furthermore, you work in a competitive environment not just externally but also internally. Your colleagues and you are often compared to each other and you're competing with them to get the monthly or quarterly mention.

Your fears around doing this including fear of rejection, fear of failure, fear of the unknown and fear of being judged could be getting in the way of you achieving great results from your interactions with others. The great news is that all of these can be overcome through this system. You will have hard proven strategies and techniques to interact with and influence people that will not only be easier but also way more effective.

And finally, to nurture and get the best out of every **PROSPECT** whilst also getting both them and you the results, I train my clients on **The AIM to Claim Principle™.**

Successful recruiters 'map' their markets to attract highly qualified clients and adopt an approach that allows them to work on a captive segment that brings them the results. Six-figure recruiters do not try to cover everything that's out there, otherwise there is a danger of spreading yourself too thin.

For example, if you recruit in the marketing sector, going after everything marketing-led is like recruiting for the universe. There is a whole lot out there! For example, there is the client side, agency, digital, B2B, consumer, product…the list can go on.

By taking time to analyse the market, you recognize which areas emerge as lucrative, in which areas more candidates are available, which area gives a better return for your time and effort, and areas where competition isn't as tough. In addition, mapping the market gives you better leverage at becoming an expert in a specific area. This means candidates and clients will come to you because you're seen as the expert in that sector, so you'll be considered as having the most lucrative network of contacts. It gets you closer to the action and you're always in the know when people are leaving and people are being promoted. You'll be able to follow your candidates and clients as they move from company to company.

This module ultimately gives you the tools to map out a strategy that you can aim for and give you a market and client-base you can claim!

'The Mind is everything. What you think, you become'.

BUDDHA

THE RECRUITER'S PSYCHOLOGY - THE MIND MANAGEMENT MAP™

| **Chapter 5 -** The Recruiter's Psychology – The Mind Management Map™ |

The one thing every recruiter must have to be the best in the industry is the ability to bounce back from rejection, unexpected turns, last minute set backs and fallouts. By adopting the techniques from this book, some of the above will decrease, while some of these things will still happen. It's a bit like life and candidates and clients are like the chocolates in a box. You just never know which one you'll get.

The right mindset simply allows you to look at some of these challenging times in your career with a different lens and see a different perspective. Being able to get back up and keep going is a common and much-needed trait in recruitment. Having the ability to learn from past experiences, past failures and past setbacks and evaluate yourself on how you can do things differently next time is at the core of every great, successful recruiter.

Learning and understanding this module will ultimately take you through three key parts:

| **COMMUNICATE** |

The Communications Model – How to get a better understanding of the way every individual interprets things. Recognise patterns in the way they communicate with us.

| **CAPTIVATE** |

How to keep yourself and others motivated. How to tap into your clients' and candidates' motivations and be able to influence them more effectively.

| **CREATE** |

How do people operate and think internally? What makes them come to the decisions they do and how can you understand this? And, more importantly, how can you change your perception and judgment so you can deal with clients and candidates with more of an open mind? Only you can create your success.

A closer look at how you can have all of this at your core,

| Neuro Linguistic Programming (NLP) |

There are lots of names given to describe the study of Neuro Linguistic Programming. My favourites over the years include 'Jedi mind tricks' and 'Voodoo magic.' What is interesting is that the 'look into my eyes, look into my eyes' cult, hypnotic, witchcraft approach is actually one we ALL use to some extent – without even realizing.

So what is the true definition? Well, let's break it down:

Neuro – refers the brain and the nervous systems within it
Linguistics – refers to the language
Programme – in this case refers to how the brain is programmed – through behaviours and habits

Put it this way, as individuals all of us have the same operating system. It's built the same and has the same components to make it function. It has the ability to take in a huge amount of information through our five senses – certainly more than we know what to do with and if we tried to hold everything, we would probably short circuit. So, when we take in these bits of information, it goes through a **filtering** process so we can consciously make sense of it.

The filters include such things as values, beliefs, experiences and language; all of these help us to make sense of information we take in and put a meaning to it. And it's worth noting here that as individuals, these filters are unique to us which means two people could experience the exact same event yet have a complete different perspective on it.

So, as a recruiter, let's just think about that for a moment. Two recruiters from two different agencies could interview the same candidate and see completely different things. One could dismiss the candidate as not good enough whereas the other recruiter could, if asking the right questions without judgment, uncover something else about that candidate and place him or her in a great role!

Our unique perspective is often referred to, in the NLP world, as our map of the world.

And here's the thing to learn and remember: a success-led map of the world will help us to reach our goals and dreams. But a negative one can stop us from reaching our true potential.

The study of NLP helps us to change the ineffective language we use (when communicating with others as well as ourselves) to one that is more empowering and brings about better results.

This is done by ultimately changing our limiting beliefs – the beliefs that hold us back, that keep us in our comfort zone and stop us from moving forward, the beliefs that make us cynical or judgmental – to beliefs that are more empowering and have a better influence over us and our decisions and allow us to view life and others in a more positive way.

In recruitment, it's this that makes the difference between being good and being GREAT! And the above example where recruiter two saw something more in that candidate and placed him or her is a common occurrence in the industry. Recruiter two's beliefs were less limiting. They had more of an open mind and didn't base their decision on beliefs that may have distorted their viewpoint.

| COMMUNICATE |

If how you communicated with others had a more positive influence over them, if you could convince candidates to recognise opportunities that they hadn't thought of before (because their brains were unable to recognise them), if you were able to influence clients to see recruitment from the perspective and value that you saw it from, if you were able to appreciate others and see what others missed, wouldn't that make a huge difference?

And what about you? How would it be if every time you had a day where everything you did just didn't happen as you planned, and instead of getting frustrated, angry, upset and repeating the same pattern, you were able to view it differently and try something new? Or you were able to turn around a losing situation into a winning one, simply because you were able to recognise the other person's perspective and way of thinking, tap into it and speak to them in a way that it made sense to them?

In short, NLP is ultimately, in its purest form, the ability to COMMUNICATE! With both others **and** yourself!

| A STRATEGY FOR SUCCESS |

You see, everything we do in life, we have a strategy for. The more we do it, the more second nature it becomes. Right from waking up in the morning and brushing our teeth! You don't think about it but it's a strategy that freshens you up, has you start your day, ensures your breath doesn't stink and you have good teeth for longer.

Learn the techniques that can help you adopt a more empowering psychology, eliminate your limiting beliefs within your profession, and practice them, so that this strategy for success becomes second nature.

Mastering these techniques would undoubtedly give you better results more consistently because you'd have recognised the strategy for success.

Soon, you'll be making successful placements, bringing in new clients, getting more candidates to accept jobs, and increasing your revenue; whatever the stumbling block is for you, it will no longer be in the way.

Now, if you're at all interested in personal development and using NLP and the many techniques and interventions within it that can improve your results, then as much as this this book will reveal to you some of the techniques that worked best for me and enhanced my skills as a professional recruiter and improved my financial results, it isn't a book about NLP.

If you're interested in qualifying as an NLP Practitioner and really taking yourself to another level, then I have a great bonus offer for you.

My friend Tosin Ogunnusi, who was one of my NLP coaches when I studied it, is an exceptional trainer, and has a special offer for you just because you're reading this book. Visit his website: ***www.mpowerment. co.uk*** and sign up to receive **your free** MP3 and eBook explaining all about how the mind works.

| The Communications Model |

This is, in my opinion, the foundation that underpins everything there is to know about effective communication and how you can achieve it, every time! It starts by understanding just how we make sense of all that we come across.

The Communications Model is an illustration of how we process information through various filters and respond based on the meaning we have assigned to what we have perceived.

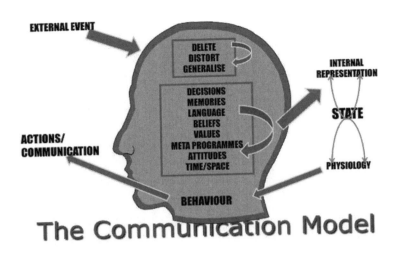

The Communication Model

So, here is what happens: we take in an experience from the outside world through our five senses: Kinesthetic (Touch), Olfactory (Smell), Gustatory (Taste), Auditory (Hear) and Visual (See). The reason it needs to be filtered through these five is so that through neurological impulses, our brains can begin to make sense of them. Co-founder of NLP John Grinder calls this "first access," a reality purely based on sensory filters. So for example, babies often operate at this level before they learn the art of language. They may accidently touch a radiator, cry and resist touching it again because it was hot. Their brains have made a neurological connection based on the fact that it was hot. That's the meaning they attached to what happens when you touch the thing that looked like a radiator.

Obviously, as we start to learn the art of language, we start to put labels on things to make meaning of them and that becomes our reality. We give each experience a meaning, an interpretation. The way we do this is by deleting, distorting and generalising the information we take in based on a number of filters which I mentioned earlier (our experiences, beliefs, values, our memories, our language etc.). All of these things help us to put our own meaning onto any experience that comes in from the outside world so that we can simply make sense of it.

Now I totally understand how complex this whole process is to understand and believe me, I could write a book on just this alone, but let me pick out the most salient points that will help you specifically in your recruitment career.

Let me go into a bit more detail on the filtering process **delete, distort** and **generalise** as this ultimately affects the way in which we communicate both within ourselves and with others.

| DELETE |

As I mentioned earlier on, we have the capacity to take in a billion pieces of information. Our unconscious mind does in fact take in a million bits of information every second but the conscious mind can only deal with 7 (+ or -) 2 things at any one time. So 'delete' doesn't mean we actually delete things from our minds forever; it simply means that we delete those things that aren't relevant otherwise our brains would pretty much fry in an attempt to notice the million things per second. So, how do we delete within language? Well, imagine meeting friends for a drink in the evening and asking them how their day had gone. Imagine if they explained every minute detail of what they had done from the moment they had woken up, including having showered and brushed their teeth, followed by their journey from the door to the station and then to work...JEEZ! We'd need a fair few more hours before they even got to what did after lunch. Of course they wouldn't do that. Well, I hope not, anyway. Instead, they would offer you a synopsis of the day and probably present a few highlights of that day that they want to share with you or get your advice on.

Deletion allows us to delete what is not relevant. You can already see the benefits. But when deletion occurs it can also cause misunderstandings or have you miss potential opportunities. Often as a recruiter, we are so in our heads wondering what to say next that we actually delete some of the information the client or candidate is giving us. Our focus is so on ourselves that our listening skills are switched off and we delete important information that could lead to more business and be the difference between making a placement and not.

| DISTORT |

Secondly, we **distort**. When we distort things, what we're essentially doing is making them fit into our reality.

Then we repeat it the way that we'd like it to be rather than the way it is. We basically distort the way we take things in from the outside world. So for example, in recruitment you may have two consultants interviewing the same candidate and they will come out with completely different opinions of that one particular candidate. If you are able to take away your preconceived ideas, you may be able to notice potential in your candidates that you wouldn't otherwise. So, if they've been ignored by every other competitive agency, it works to your advantage because you've noticed something that they didn't and been able to sell them in and get them their dream job.

| GENERALISE |

The third and final thing we do is **generalise**. There are a number of reasons why generalisation can be a good thing in recruitment, but also something that could stop you from being as successful as you could be. So here's the good news first: it's important that we generalise because if we didn't, every time we did the same task we would have to learn it from scratch. So for example, every time we bought a new car if we didn't generalise we would have to learn to drive it from the beginning. In the same way, every time a job came in from a client we would have to learn the whole recruitment process from scratch. Generalisation allows us to make sense of things based on previous experience. Now for the not so good news: generalisation is also the reason that prejudices and biased opinions are formed. In the early stages of your recruitment career when you're learning to make sales calls and the first two or three don't go as planned, you make a generalisation that you're not good at it. An opinion gets formed that it's something that you're not good at and you don't like which then becomes your reality. This affects all future calls because of the generalisation you've made. Even the language that you use dictates that. For example: always, everyone, every time, never. All of these words indicate that you've made an internal opinion about something that cannot be changed.

All three of the above filters have their place and it's because of these three that we have continued to evolve as professionals. However, if you're not aware of what these three filters actually do, they can also prevent you from being successful and realising your true potential.

So, once we have filtered an event or experience by deleting, distorting and generalising, based on our previous decisions, memories, beliefs, and values, we make an internal **representation.**

What do I mean by an internal representation? Basically, we apply a meaning to it. And when we put a meaning to it, depending what the meaning is, it has a direct impact on our **emotional state** and **physiology.**

Let's put this in context.

For example: A call between you and a client doesn't go as well as you hoped. You create a meaning based on your filtering system and it's a negative one. You believe you weren't good; you think you've said something wrong. You believe it means you're not good at your job, not good at selling, and you feel rejected (emotional state). Your emotions turn to you feeling uncomfortable, upset, angry, nervous, and anxious. This then changes your physiology, your body language.

When this happens, it creates behaviour that then leads to and has a direct impact on your action or communication thereafter. In the example we have used above, it may affect your next call if you've internally created the meaning that you aren't good at cold-calling. Or, you may take it out on your team. Or, you may generalise and feel ALL clients are a waste of time. Or, you may feel less confident during your next call because you're afraid of being judged or think you're not good enough.

This is often referred to as a 'pattern of behaviour' because the more you continue the same behaviour, it becomes ingrained within your neurology, thus becoming a pattern you run every time you go through the same experience. Each time you have a negative experience with a client, you repeat the same behaviour and this eventually becomes your limiting belief, instilled stronger each time.

So let me ask you this: If you were to change your internal representation to be one that was more positive, which had a positive effect on your state/physiology, do you think this would change your behaviour that would ultimately lead to a more positive action? Absolutely.

| Beliefs |

The only way you can consider changing the meaning you put to things is to change your beliefs. Have beliefs that serve you better, that are more empowering. By changing your beliefs, attitude and decisions, you create better meanings; by creating better meaning, you create a better state; a better state leads to a better behaviour that ultimately leads to better actions and/or communications.

However, for many, it's more comfortable to hold on to the old belief, the belief that stops you from succeeding and realising your true potential. Staying there is safer and less challenging. And more importantly, it gifts you all the excuses you need for why it didn't work. You tried, it didn't work, and it wasn't your fault.

At the same time, your beliefs also stop you from recognising the true potential of your candidates. Your beliefs could cloud your judgment on someone without any reason other than what you may have experienced in the past.

So, how can your beliefs compel your candidates and clients to be more motivated to work with you?

Your clients or candidates may have a negative or misleading perspective of how recruiters work, how they operate and what they're like. I am sure you've heard some of these misconceptions: Recruiters are just concerned about money, recruiters don't ever call back, they cost too much, fees are too high, all they do is supply CVs, they waste time. I am sure there are a few more you can think of.

Well, all of these are beliefs they have about you that are untrue. These beliefs are based on the experiences they've had and caused them to generalise and put all recruiters in the same box. But just like the belief you had when you were younger that Santa Claus was real has now become untrue, the beliefs about recruiters that are untrue can also be changed. And you can do that. In fact, if you are a recruiter who loves what you do, loves the industry and who believes you do a great job and give immense value to your clients and candidates, then this is something you MUST learn and be wanting to do.

Challenging the status quo

To be a game changer in your industry, you need to challenge the status quo. That's how you change beliefs. You need to challenge them and give them an alternative perspective. That's how objections are handled by successful recruiters; challenge beliefs and through the right communication, you can change the way they think and the alter the meaning they attach to recruitment so that their next action is to use you, trust you, and believe in you.

'Your past does not equal your future.'

TONY ROBBINS

Successful recruiters do the opposite. They're open to changing their beliefs, letting go of the very thing that stops them from being successful and instead taking responsibility for their own success and the path towards it. Successful recruiters won't have excuses but will create new solutions. Successful recruiters do not allow their past negative experiences, their past rejections, or their past failures hold them back.

This is how winning recruiters stay in the game and motivate themselves and others to maintain their success.

| CAPTIVATE |

| Language |

Now we've discussed the process of deletion, distortion and generalisation and how this is done based on a number of filters as shown in the Diagram. One of the filters used in this process and that is paramount to being successful in any sales-based career and especially in recruitment, is language.

I can hear you ask, "what exactly do you mean by language?" I mean, don't we all speak English (or whatever your country's official language is)? Ever sent an email and the recipient has taken the wrong end of the stick?

We just proved this happens in the explanation of The Communications Model; even when you speak the same language (literally), how we understand each other differs. We make our own interpretations based on what we believe, our past experiences, and our conditioning. We put our own meaning to it.

Understanding how others think and appealing to their way of communicating contributes highly to the success of a recruiter and certainly did with me. Learning the different ways people communicate through the words they use allowed me to not just change the way I communicated back to them, but helped me to recognize certain cues conversationally that gave me the insight needed to deal with different people and motivate and engage with them. This helped me in all areas of my career: how to motivate teams I managed, how to influence clients and candidates more effectively, how to turn "no" and "I'll think about it" into "YES!" I did this simply by speaking their language. So let's look at some examples in a little more detail to learn how to do this.

| We're all programmed! |

Over time, our neurology has been programed to communicate in a certain way. Our experiences, values, and beliefs all affect the way we communicate. The way we have been programmed guides us on how best to interact with the world around us, helping us to make sense of the information that comes to us so we know how best to respond, communicate and behave externally.

Now these aren't personality-dependent; our external response and behaviour can change dependent on the environment or context we are in. For example, how we behave with work colleagues or work situations could be and is likely to be completely different from how we are at home with the family or when we're with friends.

The great thing is, to be able to identify how someone is programmed and therefore tap into his or her way of thinking, there are a number of patterns in conversation that you need to recognize. Once you learn to look out for them, either in others or in yourself, you can motivate, influence, and communicate with them appropriately.

| CREATE |

This last part of **The Mind Management Map** underpins everything you have learned so far. The truth is that if you want to be successful at anything, you have to create your own success. Make success be your reality. I can give you all the techniques and tips in this book on how to be a successful recruiter, but there is only one person who can make it happen. And there is only one person who can hold you back...

The choice is yours.

Internal Dialogue – the conscious and unconscious

Let me ask you this: Do you talk to yourself? Of course you do, we all do. And it's completely normal. Some of us do it internally and some of us talk out loud. You may even be sat next to a colleague who suddenly says something and when you ask if they were talking to you; they tell you they were simply thinking out loud.

Although not measurable, there have been lots of informal statistics around how much we actually do talk to ourselves. Apparently, as a minimum it's at least over 50% of our waking life, and the only times that we don't actually do it is if we are completely focused on a specific thing (like reading a book or watching television). It is during these focused times that we are able to switch off that voice inside of us.

When we do talk to ourselves we're engaging the conscious mind; it's this conscious mind that interacts with the unconscious mind, eventually embedding whatever we are saying to ourselves deep within the brain.

Let's take a moment to think about this. If what we say to ourselves is consistently negative, telling ourselves that we're not good at this or we can't do that, eventually the unconscious mind will form a connection inside of us (in our neurology, to be precise) so we eventually believe it to be true.

The key to success is to integrate the unconscious and conscious so that they are better aligned with one another.

We can use the communication skills and language that we have already discussed to ensure they speak to each other in a more empowering way to bring about a better partnership, so that they work together as a team and not on opposite sides, so that how we are and what we do is more congruent, in line with our true values. You can transform your beliefs to better serve you.

| Cause or Effect |

What often holds people back from reaching success depends on which side people 'live,' **Cause or Effect.** So, what do I mean by this?

'Cause or effect' is the difference between taking responsibility for what happens to you and doing something about it, or believing things always happen 'to you.' Let's examine these two types of people in the world more closely.

Those who live at 'cause' take responsibility and can recognise choices they have made. Living at cause makes you decisive and accountable for your results and achievements. You see opportunity and take actions to seize these opportunities. You react to things in an empowering way and when one way doesn't work, you have the ability to see alternative possibilities. You find other solutions.

If you live life at 'effect' blame is where you turn first. You look to blame others or blame circumstances when things don't go the way you want. You wait and hope for things to turn out right and when they don't, you become the victim. It's never your fault and as a result you can't see beyond this to notice the possibilities and opportunities that are available.

Recruiters can often fall into this very situation and when this occurs the potential of their success is reduced drastically. It's an easy trap to fall into. Maybe the economy is bad, the candidate is unreliable, there aren't any good candidates left in the market, the client doesn't know what he or she wants, a colleague persuaded the candidate to take his job, the company doesn't have the resources, I haven't been given the job board I want, I have a database of bad clients, he/she has all the good clients, there is too much competition in my sector, the sector isn't recruiting... and on and on it goes. Sound familiar? There are probably a whole lot more that I haven't even mentioned.

I lived at effect for a long time; it was easier to blame something else than take accountability and responsibility. If I didn't do great at my exams, it was because of my health or because I didn't have a good teacher. When I didn't make it as a journalist, it was simply because there wasn't enough support and guidance around to help me in that career choice. When I couldn't lose weight it was because of my diabetes. There was always something and, in my recruitment career, when I had bad months it was due to market conditions, bad candidates, and bad management.

I was ready to give up on my recruitment career two years after I started when we hit the 2001 recession, the digital bust. Companies stopped recruiting in the numbers they had done before, the company I was working for restructured and laid off staff that, although I survived, left me under immense pressure. There were management changes, increased KPIs, micro-management and aggressive tactics. I didn't like the industry anymore as it was taking me away from where I was comfortable (a place where clients called in, candidates were great and the market was buoyant).

It was hard and all of the above excuses were preventing me from succeeding.

Through the study and understanding of human behaviour I learned one key thing:

'Everything we need to be highly successful is within us'

STEPHEN R COVEY

If you want to be happy, sad, poor, rich, successful or a failure, the choice is in your hands. And this substantial revelation is crucial if you want to embark on a sales-orientated career. It is imperative to master in order to be successful in recruitment.

The truth is, there are no bad circumstances, only bad recruiters. Harsh, I know...but true. But it's not all bad news! If you can move yourself away from effect and over to cause, you'll change your perspective and your results. That's what transforms average or good recruiters into great ones. And the great news is, those of you who have been living at effect – with a bit of work, coaching and support – you can easily make your way over to the other side.

| TAKEAWAYS... |

- You are not defined or paralysed by your old beliefs. You can create new ones.
- Everyone has his or her own "map of the world" and you simply need to tap into it to understand people better.
- What you think about, you bring about.
- Focus goes where energy flows – so begin to focus on what you can do.
- Take accountability for your own results – only you can change your results.
- A FEAR is simply False Evidence Appearing Real. You can alter your own reality

Our deepest fear is not that we are inadequate.
Our deepest fear is that we are powerful beyond measure.
It is our light not our darkness that most frightens us
Your playing small does not serve the world.

Marianne Williamson

'I have always said that everyone is in sales. Maybe you don't hold the title of salesperson, but if the business you are in requires you to deal with people, you, my friend, are in sales'.

ZIG ZIGLAR

CHAPTER 6
PROCESS

| **Chapter 6 -** Process |

So, now you have the tools to ensure you instill the right mindset, attitude and approach. You know what it takes to be effective with your communication both with yourself and others in order to obtain a successful outcome. You have the perfect foundation and perspective to grasp the RECRUITMENT process.

The Placement P.R.O.F.I.T. Generator™ will guide you through from A to Z, or in this case, from the P to T of recruitment.

| **PERSUADE** |

I remember clearly how I NEVER wanted to work in sales. As far as I was concerned, I wasn't good at it and it wasn't a career I planned on pursuing. To me, salespeople were those who knocked on your door, stopped you in the street or called you on your phone at the most inconvenient times. And they were all about forcing you to buy something you didn't want or need. My *belief* was you had to have balls to be successful in sales and get the sale in the end regardless of how your customer feels.

So it's quite ironic that I was only 14 when I first began working in sales, and continued to work in sales after university. After exiting the world of journalism, I once again found my niche in sales! Yes, whatever label you give it, recruitment is ultimately all about selling. Although when I first began in this career, I didn't see it that way, simply because of what my perception of salespeople was. And even when I started in the recruitment industry, I still couldn't bring myself to admit that what I did was sell. Nope! I was in an industry that helped people find jobs and clients find people.

Then Jeremy, a senior manager in my first job, got me to see the word differently. If you'd been with me back in 1999, you would have been sat next to me in a training room with this short, red-haired individual with a big personality. "Raise your hand if you believe you work in sales." Not me, my hand is staying well and truly down. "Nooo, that's not what we do, keep your hands down," I thought to myself as I watched some of my colleagues raise their hands.

That's when Jeremy spoke. "If you don't embrace the fact you're in sales – you wont be helping very many people for much longer. How will you serve the people we are dealing with? If you don't sell your services to clients – how will your candidates ever have any opportunities to consider?" it was at that moment, I had a 'PING' moment! For the first time, I was happy to say I worked in sales!

| Why do people buy? |

All buying decisions are based on four key emotions. These four things get people to buy and as long as we cover all four areas, those purchasing feel like they have made the right decision and can avoid feeling buyer's remorse.

When these emotions are addressed and your client still decides not to buy, that's OK because, for whatever the reason, it just isn't the right time for him or her, or your service isn't one he or she currently needs.

But, if they buy, as a salesperson, you are NOT selling them anything they don't want. Instead, you're giving them exactly what they NEED. You're providing them with a solution to their problem

This saves you from feeling that you're coming across as manipulative or insincere and forcing people to buy into something they don't want. These are emotions often felt by recruiters that ultimately prevents them from helping people and at the same time increasing their revenue.

So, let me explain these four stages of emotions that get people to buy.

Client Closing Quadrant™

PAIN: The first thing you need to do is help them discover their pains (problems / struggles) and connect with them. Now, before you ask… we're not talking about projecting what you think their PAIN is onto them. What I mean by this is you need to ask enough questions to help your client discover what is missing, what it is they need that you can provide. Help them to become aware of the challenges recruiting themselves would give them, or how much having a vacant position would cost them. These challenges or pains may be different for each client. It's your job to help them discover theirs and bring it to the forefront. How can you turn the dial and perhaps outline the consequences if these problems remain?

Once you have done that, you can move onto the next stage:

PROSPECT: Once you have discovered their problem, you don't want to leave them there; you want to reveal a solution that moves them towards their end result, an optimistic outlook that demonstrates that there is a direction they can take and move towards. Make this a specific picture in their head. For example, a happier and more complete workforce allows them to focus on the strategic elements of their role, positions filled mean that sales targets will be met/exceeded, profits will be made and projects completed. What is the ideal prospect for your client's future?

Now, the third element of the quadrant is really important, as you need to be able to show your client the connection between this second point and your position.

POSITION: You now need to demonstrate that you are the one person that can solve this for them. And remember, even if you're working for a bigger agency, in recruitment, people do business with people they like and trust – so you need to show them why you. If you don't show a link between you and their future prospect, then they will absorb your suggested solution and go with the next recruiter that calls in; the next recruiter won't have to do much to get the business. But guess what? You did all the hard work!!! You just failed to demonstrate that YOU were the crucial link!

So, in this step they need to believe you're the only person who understands them and can resolve their pains. This is where you demonstrate what similar clients you have worked with, competitors you've worked with, results you've achieved, guarantees you can give them, resources you have on hand to approach their target market and contacts they may not have access to.

This is where your credibility and expertise should come into play in order to position you as the answer.

Throughout your career, you need to ensure you have testimonials and blog endorsements that you can share. Demonstrate your expertise via speaking events, videos and content marketing. You need social proof. Ensure your position holds weight, giving you credibility, authority and visibility – making you the trusted partner to work with.

Now make note that once you address the above three, your client may still not move to making a decision. The last part is ensuring a **Call to Action** in order to:

PROGRESS: Even with everything you have just done, clients can still walk away with an "I'll think about it," or, "call me in a month's time" answer. This is usually because having to make a change and decision doesn't come easily to many. And it's up to you to help them progress past the last hurdle especially if you have discovered there is a need that you can serve. Think about your successful client wins. What was the turning point that prompted a YES from them? Had their current plans not yielded anything yet? Other recruiters not come up trumps? Did you have someone you could immediately talk to them about? What was stopping them from progressing? Was their revenue stagnant because they didn't have the right person in place? Was there pressure from the CEO to get it sorted out? Think of things where, for your client, there needed to be a change in order for them to get the result they want. And remind them of it!

| KEY TO SUCCESSFUL PERSUASION |

A lot of my success in recruitment came from understanding what exactly selling was. I'd always thought of it as something unethical, forced, and manipulative. Changing my perspective changed my result.

Persuading, Influencing and Convincing: A survey carried out in the US, Europe and UK by Daniel Pink, author of To Sell is Human, discovered that 1 in 9 people in the workforce had the word sales in either their job title or job description. It's certainly a high ratio; however, delving deeper, something more interesting was uncovered about the remaining 8 in 9; they actually spent 41% of their time 'persuading, influencing and convincing' others to exchange one thing for something else.

Without selling there would be so much more that we wouldn't achieve. We wouldn't ever be able to get a job, employ someone, find a life partner, date, be a great parent, treat a patient, or save an innocent person.

You see, selling is part of human existence and we're doing it all the time. In order to get your dream job you sell yourself, your skills and your expertise in an interview to convince and influence their decision. When you date, from the moment you first meet them to every date thereafter, you're selling your personality, your values, your likes and dislikes, and your faults in the hope they fall for you. Parents have to influence their children to take the right path, children persuade their parents to let them have an extra half hour before bed. Doctors often need to convince their patients of the right treatment for their ailment, even if the patient would rather not have it and they then have to sell security and assurance to the patient to convince them everything will be OK. I could go on but I think you have the point…

I carried out a survey on LinkedIn asking recruiters to grade what they liked best about their job. New business development and selling came last. More often than not, this is because they just have a misperception of selling. They have fears around doing it: fear of rejection, fear of failure, and fear of being wrong.

I discovered an easy and efficient formula that helped me overcome this limiting thinking, which I am about to share.

www.viamii.com/training

Remember, selling is in every part of our role; yes, we have to sell our service to new clients and convince them to use us. But we also have to sell jobs to candidates, salaries to both clients and candidates, people to clients, and opportunities to candidates. So, why is it that recruiters love one side of selling (to candidates) but not the other (business development)?

Well, to help my clients grasp the art of selling and achieve great results, they learn **The C-Section Selling Blueprint™**. It's a simple, yet effective process that helps recruiters ultimately get business with new clients without feeling uncomfortable or as if they are reading a script. This framework works regardless of which industry you recruit for as the content of the framework is filled by questions and statements relevant to your industry. That's where you become the expert in your field instead of a pushy salesperson. So, let's take a look at these steps more closely.

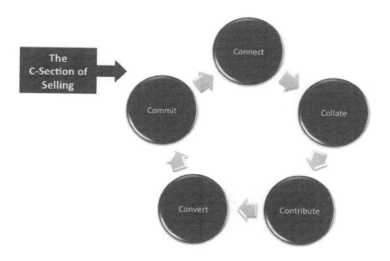

Connect: Whether you're at a client meeting or speaking to them over the phone, you need to establish a connection with them. Building rapport may have already been done over the phone so, if in a meeting, this is your chance to strengthen that using body language. (We'll explore that more in the next section). The other crucial part to this stage is setting the tone of the meeting or call from the start – and you need to be the one that does that first – take control.

Let's take a look at how:

- Smile – It works every time.
- Find an area of common interest, build rapport, check their LinkedIn, uncover something useful and interesting about them.
- Take time to start building the relationship instead of just launching into a business exchange
- Be the one to introduce an agenda. Offer what you think will be useful to cover.

Collate: Here is where your expertise comes into crucial play. It's time to find out about them, their business, their needs, their pains etc. You don't want to bombard them with irrelevant questions because remember, ask quality questions and you'll get quality answers. So make them count – especially if you have limited time. Useful questions to ask in order to establish long-term understanding would be to understand their department / practice / business, so you can use this information to sell back to candidates. Find out what's important to the business, as this helps you to then match the USPs of your agency. If you're going to be discussing a position, then before you go onto that, there are three key areas you want to explore about your client:

- Overall Business
- Culture
- Recruitment Process and Supplier Service

Think about what kind of questions you would ask under the above to get a deeper understanding of your client in order to give you the best chance of filling their vacancy as well as position yourself as a long-term supplier.

You would then move onto discussing the job profile, which we cover later in the book.

Contribute: My favourite bit! This is your opportunity to sell yourself, but why does it come under the heading 'contribute'? Well, before you launch into your sales pitch you need to stop and consider what you have extracted from your clients. Then sell to them the relevant parts of your service.

One technique to consider here is 'seeding.' This is when you subtlety drop facts to demonstrate that you understand their challenges by mentioning how you may have dealt with them elsewhere.

You do this swiftly and concisely providing a reference but not labouring the point as if in casual conversation. Plant a seed of relevancy. Naturally, even though you are conversational, you are ultimately still pitching.

It's worth noting here that this section where you get to pitch should be the shortest part of the process. Why? Because you should have been 'seeding' the sale from the moment you started talking to them.

This then takes us to…

Convert: Time to summarise and cover any last-minute points and ask for the business! Agree on terms and fees. When it comes to reducing fees, here is where you would explain how reduced fees are not in your interest or the clients.

As a recruiter, let me ask you, could your willingness to reduce fees represent a lack of confidence or faith in your ability? Remember not to de-value the service you provide by reducing fees easily. After all, people get what they pay for. How important is it for the client that their recruitment process has your FULL attention? Well, why would you give it priority if the reward does not match the work you put into it?

Commit: This piece is usually the one that is missed out and when it is, it can often mean you lose control of the client and the process. This section is all about managing the client, the process and the client's expectations.

Gain commitment from your client by agreeing on a Service Level Agreement (SLA) of the plan moving forward. Agree in advance on dates and timelines for interview dates. Suggest that they interview on your agency's premises, where there is no distraction and interviews can take place all in one day. Or, agree on timelines for when you will hear back once you have sent CVs or candidates have been interviewed.

(If you hadn't done this before, you want to make sure they are the decision maker and, if not, find out who else is involved.)

One of my very first clients gained from my own new business development was a technology-based content agency based outside London (Aylesbury). They recruited for Technical Editors and their brief was very specific due to the kind of work they did.

CHAPTER 6 – PROCESS

So, challenges that I faced already included location, sector and tightness of brief. I suggested they interview in London for the first interview so that it was easier for people to attend a first, especially if they were currently working in London. They loved the idea and so we put a date in the diary, which meant I had something concrete to work towards but more than that, it meant I was the only specialist recruiter they used.

It was up to me to get the best 3-5 people shortlisted and selected for that date. Even though I did still have to send CVs to them beforehand to select, it also meant that if someone last minute dropped out, I could make a decision based on my knowledge of the client's requirements, to slot someone in last minute that they may not have selected.

On the day of interview, after each candidate was met with, I had full control of the process. I got immediate feedback from the candidate and client and at the end of the day was able to confirm second round interviews with those candidates who were interested and eliminate those candidates who weren't. This also meant my client's time was saved, as I was able to instantly inform them if a candidate they were interested in was a "no."

This process led to a guaranteed placement and a very happy client and candidate. And it worked each time I did it.

To master the art of persuasion and be able to sell successfully, comfortably and enjoyably, use this process and your results will start coming in!

| Climb into B.E.D. |

OK, so not literally! But always remember – whether you are selling to candidates or clients, do this one thing and you'll find selling is an art.

First, you need to:

Believe: You must change your beliefs about what selling is and why you do it. Replace the word 'sales' with 'influence' and it brings a whole new meaning to it. Influence helps those who are stuck make a choice. If someone doesn't have a need, they will NEVER buy your product or service. But when you identify a need, all you're doing is influencing them to use you because you're the right consultant or agency for them. There is no force, just reinforcement – they have the need, remember.

And for those who are sitting on the fence, you simply influence them in making a decision. The decision can go either way – use an agency or advertise direct – but at least they've made a choice. Effective recruiters, who value their role and love what they do, can influence clients and candidates to use them without force and without manipulation. Simple persuasion. And it all comes from what they believe.

Next you need to…

Empathise: whenever you're in a position to persuade or influence, it comes from one place and one place only. Even though it may be unconscious, it deeply stems from a place of CARING. You need to really care for your customer, their business, their career, their development, and their growth. If you don't care, then what you sell has no value. When you begin to empathise with those you do business with, how you sell transforms and so do your results. The value you add to your client or candidate becomes transparent and before you know it, your relationship becomes a partnership.

And finally ensure you…

Deliver what you promise. Selling only becomes unethical, invaluable and immoral if what you deliver does not match the quality you sold it at. This industry suffers from a reputation created by the few cowboy (or girl) recruiters who don't deliver what they say they will. Managing your client and candidate expectations from the offset and ensuring that you (excuse the cliché), 'under promise and over deliver' raises your profile immensely.

Get into B.E.D. and it'll smell like roses.

It's simple:

> **'Take the myths about selling out of your mind, and persuade your clients that you're the best recruiter they'll ever find'.**
>
> *DEENITA PATTNI*

| RAPPORT |

Building rapport is a fundamental technique not used by enough recruiters. Those who use it not only build better relationships in the moment but also ensure that business connections stay strong years down the line. And because most of our work is done over the phone, rapport building is often forgotten about. Just before we phone a client or candidate, we are in our own heads, thinking about what we are going to say in order to get the business.

Before we look at how we can build rapport instantly (given that in our profession we only have moments to do so), let me explain rapport in more detail.

Rapport is the ability to connect with another individual based on common ground, similarities, and goals. When you have rapport with someone there is a connection, a liking that occurs and a sense of familiarity. But I believe it's more than that. Rapport is caring about your candidate/client, caring about what you do and caring about others enough to provide them with value. And you know what the great thing about that is? When you care, you build rapport instantly. It becomes more than just a technique...it becomes a way of being.

In business, the need to build rapport instantly is vital especially if you're trying to win over a client, candidate or contract. There are times when you're having to pitch to a room seated with four or five decision makers and you only have 15 minutes to get them to like you. I know. I've been there. Building rapport with all of them will hold you in good standing especially if you're up against other agencies that have been invited to pitch too.

Presentations may appear similar, but building rapport and connecting will get them to see you differently from your competitors.

Now you may be thinking, surely building rapport happens over time so how does this work when you don't have time?

The great news is that there are techniques that can be used to speed up the process to show your client just how much you care about their business and therefore want to win it.

There are three ways in which you can build rapport. Through your physiology, otherwise known as your body language, through your voice quality, and through the words you say. Albert Mehrabian developed a model allocating a percentage of effectiveness to each of these three channels. A mistake that many recruiters (and, in fact, many salespeople) make is believing that what they say to clients is the most effective way to build rapport and so they focus intensely on this area. Ironically, this is the weakest way to do so and instead you should use your physiology and your voice quality to get a higher return on your investment.

You see, building rapport through what you say is the least effective, whereas physiology is the most. And if you take physiology out of the equation (after all, a big proportion of your role is on the phone), building rapport through your voice becomes even more powerful.

So, to be more influential and get the results you want, you have to stop worrying about what you say and more about how what you say can be delivered.

And the way you use any or all of these three (words, physiology and voice quality) to build rapport is via a technique better known as matching and mirroring.

| Matching and Mirroring |

Matching and Mirroring is the behaviour of copying another individual to create and enhance a bond, a connection, and a liking with them. Interestingly enough, this actually happens naturally in social interaction. Matching and Mirroring can be done in several ways, by copying hand gestures, body movements, muscle tensions, breathing, tone, speed, accents, words, and eye movements.

Body language: Now when it comes to body language, you can match/mirror a number of things:

- Body Posture / Gestures
- Eye contact
- Blinking
- Breathing
- Smiling

Of course you want to make sure that when matching hand gestures you're not doing so when only they are speaking – as that would look a little strange. And matching aspects such as blinking you would do by using a different part of your body – such as tapping your finger each time they blink. This is often known as *cross-over matching.*

Tonality:
- Speed
- Volume
- Accents
- AVK (Auditory/Visual/Kinaesthetic)

Words:
- Paraphrasing/repeating
- Identifying your client's preferred language (Auditory, Visual, Kinaesthetic) – and speaking it

So, how does this actually help in the world of recruitment? Well, there can be a reluctance by clients to use agencies. This often comes from an ignorance or misperception of what it is we do. If you could change that perception more easily by building rapport, by addressing the misperception, you can move the client to see things from your viewpoint. And you don't need to do this by selling to them. You can do this by educating them.

Just think: if caring and education became your way of doing business, how different would the recruitment industry be viewed from how it is now. Think about how different your results would be.

So, be ready to show your clients and candidates you care. Take the industry you're passionate about and share its benefits with your client. Show them why you care about what you do.

'Building rapport on its own is a technique; combine it with caring, it will make you unique'.

DEENITA PATTNI

In any sales environment, even when you follow the techniques discussed earlier, you will always come across this next element and this is where recruiters often stumble (especially if they don't have rapport).

Where recruiters go wrong is by being afraid to tackle these head on; instead they shy away from them or pretend they don't exist which makes it harder to deal with them when they arise.

| OVERCOME |

Handling objections is, in my opinion, a sure sign of interest. Why? Because curiosity is what often brings about questions and objections are ultimately a series of questions, a series of "what if?" and the only time you'd want to ask these, is when you want to know more.

If you get an objection, it's basically something that wasn't covered in your initial chat, pitch or sales spiel and therefore an opportunity to continue the conversation.

So, when you do eventually overcome objections what you have done, in its simplest form, is take their concern and reframe it, put a different perspective or spin on it, and get them to look at it differently. You change an old BELIEF they may have had and get them to see it differently. You REFRAME them.

When you reframe something, an objection in this case, what you ultimately do is change its meaning – and this leads to changing minds. So, in sales, you can change the way your client/candidate views things by offering a different perspective.

Imagine you have a painting on your wall and for some reason it doesn't stand out; you change the frame around it and suddenly – it looks different. It tells a different story. This is the same thing.

The three types of reframing I use are easy and can often be thought of on the spot. Better still, one of them allows you to tackle potential objections before they come up – thus answering the objections whilst they're still in the client's mind. You see, your client or candidate is so ready to present their objection (after all it's a pattern they use often), that when you pre-empt the objection, you've interrupted their flow. This immediately changes the direction they were going in and gets them to reroute.

What this does is open their minds to possibilities, which means a greater chance of them saying YES.

So, let's take a look at the three types of framing before I share my framework for overcoming objections with you.

Pre-frame: This is when you would raise the objection beforehand during your conversation. For example, at the point of discussing fees, "Now Mr. Client, before I tell you my fees, I must warn you, they're not on the low side."

Context Reframe: Give another meaning to the reframe itself by changing the context.

Eg: I totally understand your concerns about our high fees, but I'm sure you would agree, that if you want the best, like a Rolex or your top of the range favourite car, you would pay for it.

Content (Meaning) Reframe: Giving another meaning to the objection by seeing what else it could mean.

Eg: I am sure the fees seem high and you may have in the past paid high fees and not received quality services. In business, when fees are reduced, often recruiters have to make a choice of where they send their best candidates and so opt to send them to the client who will give them the best return for work done. I am sure you would prefer to be the first choice for best candidates.

Once you know the three ways to reframe, how you deliver the reframe is also important:

| The Reason Reframe™ |

There are four steps to how you deliver your reframe when you're handling objections.

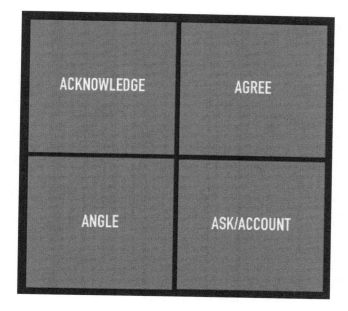

Acknowledge: Acknowledge your client/candidate's objection and empathise. Don't just dismiss it as being wrong.

Angle: Present to them a different perspective (using one of the three types of reframes).

Ask / Agreement: Ask them whether they agree or get agreement from them on your angle. This is your test close along the way because small agreements lead to big agreements, which is ultimately what you want them to do at the end.

Account: If needed, give them supporting evidence; present an account of a previous client/situation/experience where an objection they expressed was proved to be untrue.

Tip: Take a moment to consider what objections you may come across and see how you could **PRE-FRAME** those in your pitch to handle them. Alter the content of your pitch to include them.

| FILTER |

In my years within the sector, I experienced many colleagues and members of my team falling at the last hurdle, candidates rejecting job offers. Yet when I looked at my record, if I got someone to final interview stage, it was almost always a sure-fire placement. So, what was I doing that others weren't? Through training and development, as well as assessing my own success, I realised it always came down to this element: Candidate Filtering.

So, what do I mean by filtering? Well, when you interview candidates whether over the phone or in person, what you're ultimately going through is a filtering process, separating the good from the great, the brilliant from the average.

www.viamii.com/training

Interviewing candidates is a core element and contributor to ensuring a smooth placement. Managing their expectations, understanding their needs and knowing what they want is paramount to having exceptional candidate control – to the point that throughout the process of submitting them for a role, you know their moves, motives and moods.

And controlling candidates, in order to help guide them through their career choices whilst ensuring the right placement for your client, starts at the interview stage (not as some recruiters do, at the job interview stage). It's that old known adage, when you get it right from the start, it saves time and energy and avoids last minute disappointment at the end of the recruitment cycle. It also gives you room to prepare for any setbacks early on.

Mistakes made by recruiters at interview stage include:
- Only interviewing them for a specific position (therefore missing other crucial bits of information)
- Lack of probing
- Losing control of the interview
- Accepting the first answer candidates give
- Not managing candidate expectations
- Writing notes on candidate's CVs

Making these mistakes won't be realised until you get to the offer stage – when the candidate rejects the offer – usually due to a reason you could have uncovered earlier on. As a manager, when I trained my team on the **S.E.L.E.C.T. & Elect Profiler™**, their offer-to-placement ratio increased to the point at which they could have accepted on behalf of their candidate without them knowing and guaranteed a placement. So, with that, I took the teachings and now include this framework when teaching my recruitment clients.

Let's take a closer look at this: **S.E.L.E.C.T. & Elect Profiler™**

Start off by setting the **SCENE.**

It's important that YOU set the scene right from the start in a positive and welcoming way. It doesn't matter what's happening elsewhere, whether deals have been rejected, if you've had a team challenge or you're having a bad day, when you meet your candidate, you have to make them feel at ease, welcome them and convince them they are in great hands. They need to know that as their recruiter, you will take an interest in them and their needs and really listen to them.

There are a number of ways to do this (we have already covered rapport), but smaller things also have a huge effect, like smiling and finding common interests on their CV. I mean if I was to ask you how often you take notice of the interests and hobbies on their CVs, very few would say "all the time" and, if you do, many of you wouldn't be taking advantage of why this is key.

Chatting about personal interests will instantly get them to relax and be more themselves in interview. Breaking down the barriers allows you to see the real them and allows them to open up more to you, which means you get more information without trying too hard.

The other important thing when setting the scene is going over what will be involved and the timeframe. Often, candidates visit recruiters during their lunchtime and if that's the case, check in with them. How long do they have? Reveal the reason for wanting to meet, how it will benefit them, and what you will cover.

Being transparent allows for instant rapport and paves the path to building trust. When they feel like you care, they'll also be more likely to open up and be transparent.

Once you've done this, you're ready to **EXPLORE**.

Explore - This is where you get them to walk you through their CV/career. It's important to know where to start on their CV, as some people will have years of experience whereas others have less. The key is to ensure you understand the journey they took to get from where they were to where they are now, as this can reveal their motivations and drivers to you.

For example, if their reasons for leaving each job have involved conflict with authority, you know that you'll need to delve deeper into why that happens and manage the recruitment process to avoid it happening again. Or, if you know they tend to drop their salary expectations in favour of career enhancement, this will tell you that money is not their primary driver. Also, from a commercial viewpoint, knowing how they were introduced to each role will give you information on how companies they have worked for recruit, which is market intelligence that you can follow up on at a later stage.

A common mistake many recruiters make during this step is not finding out enough information about where the candidate has worked. Or, if the candidate has worked for organisations you already have as a client or are familiar with, the easy assumption is to believe you don't need to know any more.

Big mistake! Even if you're already familiar with the company your candidate has worked for/works at, getting insight from his or her perspective becomes valuable market knowledge and will give you information you were not aware of.

Questions: In this step, it's important you ask the right questions in order to avoid the interview going on for too long or going off on a tangent. Questions allow you to extract the relevant information, lead the interview where you feel it needs to go and control the interview itself. Different types of questions serve different purposes and here I'll share these with you so you can choose the appropriate ones depending on what you want to achieve when interviewing.

Question Style	Purpose	Example
Open	To obtain specific detail/get more information.	Use the 5 Ws & How: Eg: What do you mean by that? How do you do x?
Demand Open	Used to get information in a more directive/controlling manner to gain specific detail.	Pre-frame question: Eg: Talk me through x / Show me / Explain to me / Talk to me about when…
Probing	Used to expand further on a specific area.	Eg: Can you explain x / Tell me more about x / Give me an example of x.
Direct	Used to assert and gain control and great for needing to elicit specific info about a situation/area.	Eg: Tell me specifically about x.
Evidence Based	Used when you need concrete examples of their experience. Key for recruiters. Use this and your matching skills will be more successful.	Go through the STAR – L Technique – covered in the **Rapid Recruitment Engine™**
Closed	Have a place in recruitment. Require a yes or no answer. Allows you to take back control/change the subject.	
DO NOT USE:		
Hypothetical Question		
Multiple Choice Questions		

The next step in the S.E.L.E.C.T. & Elect Profiler™ is **LEVERAGE**.

With every interview, you need to find specific information that will give you **leverage**, to be effectively used when you sell them to your clients, especially in a candidate-short market. Or when you have a candidate who doesn't match the brief 100% but has a lot to offer – gaining specific leverage will help you convince a client to see your candidate. As a recruiter, your role is to mold, shape and stretch the original brief so that you can offer a choice of candidates to the client should their ideal not exist. The following formula gives us leverage to do this:

Earlier, I mentioned the **STAR-L formula**, a popular and already established process that uncovers information that we can present to the client, convincing them that who we have is worth interviewing. The STAR-L formula has been used by many establishments, however I believe the additional fifth step (represented by the letter L) is vital.

So, what exactly is it?

| SITUATION |

Get them to tell you about a specific situation. This gives you the background information and puts the experience into context. You want to ask them about a situation that you know or think a client will want to hear about. For example, in the marketing industry, it could be "describe a time you were asked to enhance a client's social media strategy."

TASK – Once they have set the scene of the situation, you want to ask them to describe the specific task and what was required of them. When addressing a task, it may be the project itself or a presentation they had to deliver.

ACTION – It's time to get down to the details! Ask them about specific actions. What did they do to resolve a problem or perform a task? Ensure that they specify what they did specifically.

RESULT – This is naturally the next step. What results did they get and how did their actions specifically affect the outcome? Was there something they did or didn't do that would have led to a different outcome?

This next step is one that is very rarely asked but I believe that by asking this, you get the best insight about both the candidate themselves and their approach and way of thinking.

- **LEARNING** – What did they learn? What additional skills did they walk away with?

You want to do at least one STAR-L for each job as its gives you some great ammunition for selling clients in. Or, uncover a STAR-L for the relevant and recent roles.

So, you may now be thinking, how can you use the information to gain leverage and therefore an advantage? Well, if you managed to gain the right information about the job itself from the client, this is where you match the information from STAR-L to what the client asked for!

The time you spend with your candidates and information gained will mean job offer rejections come to an end!

The fourth step in the **S.E.L.E.C.T. & Elect Profiler™** is often brushed over too quickly and not enough importance is given to this step. But it is indeed this step where you get to collate information that can help you control the placement further down the line. The next step is:

| EXIT |

This step covers vital information that, when extracted in the right way, will prove to be the ACE up your sleeve when it comes to your candidate accepting your job offer.

| Reason for leaving |

If you don't do this, you should!
A common mistake made by recruiters is to ask this question only for the most recent role or to only ask it once. It's amazing what information you uncover simply by asking this question!

The answer to this question will tell what motivates your candidates to stay in a role, what their common pattern is when it comes to leaving, whether they like hierarchy or not, whether they cause conflict, whether they blame, what their ambitions are, what their values are, and the triggers that cause them unrest. This information will allow you to match the right company to the right candidate and will eliminate surprise fallouts and cash refunds.

Do this and you'll be able to help your client motivate the candidate and ensure they are long term in their business.

| "Why else?" |

You should be asking them their reasons for leaving a role more than once. Why would you do that?

The truth is, the first reason they give is very rarely the 'real' reason they wanted to leave; by asking a few times, you'll get down to the core reason. So, the phrase "why else?" is your best friend.

A survey released back in 2013 on LinkedIn revealed salary as the fifth reason for leaving a job. However, a recent 2014 survey featured in Forbes Online pushed that reason further down the pecking order to number 8. A number of other surveys carried out (RecruitLoop/Forbes/Undercover Recruiter) no longer feature salary as a Top 10 reason!

Yes, for some industries, like sales, people may quit because the salary or commission isn't high enough, as money is a key motivator for most sales professionals. Having said that, you'll find that for this group of professionals, salary won't always be the 'real' reason.

So, if you really want to be able to manage your candidate's salary expectations, understanding the real motivations for leaving is key. Because an individual's reason for leaving their job is usually driven by emotion, something, that as a recruiter, you have to learn to tap into.

| ReM.I.T.™ |

Another vital piece of information to uncover under EXIT is ReM.I.T.

What do I mean by this?

Discovering what the *Most Important Things (M.I.T.)* are to them in the next step in their careers is valuable information. This is the information that you recap just before you present the job and salary offer to them. This is the information that will counteract counter offers. This is the information that will inspire your candidates to progress and start the new chapter in their careers instead of returning to their comfort zones!

The answers you reveal from both stages within EXIT are key further along in the recruitment process when you present an offer to a candidate. This information is also key when it comes to moving on to the next stage.

Once you have set the **Scene, Explored** their experience, gained **Leverage** and uncovered their **EXIT** strategy, you come to the next step in the process called the **CASH-COUNTER.** This is the one step that many recruiters deal with too early on in the process, leaving no room to influence them if they reject your offer.

This is where the subject of money is approached, extracting both their current salary/day rate and also what they're looking for. How do you get your candidate to consider a more realistic and closer-to-the-truth salary expectation? How can you get your candidate to be happy to accept a salary less than what they currently make and still feel excited?

When you ask them the required minimum salary they will consider, very much like when you ask them their reasons for leaving, their first answer is an ideal, an answer they believe you should hear. As their recruiter, your job is to manage their expectations and get them to be more flexible depending on the roles available (especially if what they believe they're worth is over-inflated.)

Here, you can use the answers gained from the previous step to get an answer closer to the truth. How do you address them so they don't feel you're forcing them to take a lower salary?

Simple. Give them a reason WHY?

Research carried out in the book Psychology of Influence by Robert Cialdini proved that when wanting to influence individuals to a different perspective, to doing favours for you, to helping you out, as long as you gave a reason most people were happy to comply.

So, two perfect reasons are:

- This way they won't miss out on hearing about ideal opportunities from great companies that they may seriously consider regardless of salary.
- They still have the option to say "no."

This small difference helps you to have a wider range of candidates to brief, ensuring you don't miss out briefing a candidate ideal for the role (especially one who would take such a role at a lower salary!)

Reminding them that the figure they give you will determine how many doors you open for them will get them to reassess their answer. Why? Because they don't want to miss out on a potentially perfect role!

And it's OK to be transparent. Another trick here is to reassure them that it's in your interest to get them the highest salary possible – after all, the more they get, the more you get, too. But at the same time, you don't want them to miss out on a great opportunity – this is what will separate you, a recruiter who cares, from your commission-caring competition!

So, what's the reason for focusing on salary in this way? Here are three very good reasons...

1. Choice: It widens the number of roles you can brief them on.
2. Chance: If you have a position that has everything they're looking for but not paying their salary you have still created a chance to brief them, because unlike other recruiters, you dug deeper into their salary expectations during the interview stage! Recruiters who didn't explore this further missed.
3. Correct: You get a more realistic and correct salary band from the candidate (one they will actually consider).

| Counter Offers |

Once you have completed this process, there is a vital stage in this step that you MUST approach. And that is the subject of counter-offers. Now you may be thinking – why would you bring this up when you've only just met them?

The last thing you want is to get to the offer stage only to find out they've been counter offered by their current employer and have decided to stay where they are. Often, recruiters do not approach this at all (or if they do, they do so too late in the process – usually at the offer stage.) You still go through this at the offer stage, but you want to deal with it much earlier on so that it stays with them throughout the process.

Asking the following questions is a good place to start:

- What would you do if your current employer offered you the same or more money at the point you resign?
- What if it was £5-10K more?
- Have you approached your manager/company about money/progression/promotion, etc.?

This leads us to the final step, which many recruiters don't give much thought to. But just like the beginning and middle of the interview process, the end also has some gems that will provide insight. If you do this in a haphazard way, you miss the opportunity to grow your business. The last step is: TERMINATE.

Terminate brings us to all the elements you need to cover at the end of the interview. Even at this stage, there are things to cover that will give you advantage over your competitors because you'll gain better control of your candidate moving forward.

Here, you cover all the remaining details:

- **NOTICE PERIOD?**
  Knowing this will give you insight into how you need to manage a candidate once they have accepted an offer from you. In the case of a 3-month notice period, you need to explore further about how negotiable this is. There are ways to work around a 3-month notice period simply by asking some powerful, key questions.

  In addition, if they're immediately available, this gives you commercial advantage if you deal with both freelance and permanent opportunities. It's a chance to offer your clients a different option they may not have thought of in order to help them out. They will appreciate this and that will win you loyalty. It's a great way to up-sell great candidates and convince clients to consider freelance candidates whilst they find someone permanent; the chance of them eventually offering the freelance candidate the permanent role is also increased.

- **WHICH OTHER AGENCIES ARE THEY SIGNED UP WITH?**
  This information will reveal to you how fast you need to act with your best candidates and also use strategies to get exclusivity. You can discover from this information how serious your candidate is about actually moving.

- **IF A FREELANCE CANDIDATE, ARE THEY LTD CO / SOLE TRADER?**

- **WHERE ELSE ARE THEY INTERVIEWING?**
  This allows you to identify the types of roles they are succeeding at and also gives you leads to follow up. In addition, it will reveal if any of your clients are recruiting.

- **HOW FAR INTO THE PROCESS ARE THEY?**
  If your candidate is out interviewing, you really want to ask this question, as your time is valuable. It creates urgency with the right roles and helps you prioritise which candidates to focus on and which to leave on the back burner.

- **Q & A**
  By allowing them the opportunity to ask you questions, it will reveal their interview approach and the types of questions they ask.

- **FEEDBACK**
  This is always my favourite part and it's also the one thing that many recruiters find uncomfortable, especially when having to give a candidate feedback on how to improve. Whether you have to give feedback on their interview style or indeed about their hygiene (yes, I am sure you've come across needing to tell someone they need to put on deodorant!), as long as you phrase it right, give them the outcome and how it will benefit them, they'll take it the right way. There could be a simple and easy-to-overcome reason why they're being rejected after first interview, but no one has ever had the guts to tell them. You could be the difference between them getting the next job or repeating the same unknown mistake.

- **SELL YOUR AGENCY**
  DO NOT START WITH THIS! The misconception some candidates have about recruiters can be amplified when this is done at the start. Don't make this about YOU – make it about them. Build rapport before you sell to them! Make their hour-long interview count and make them feel important.

  They'll be more inclined to listen to you and hear about your company and potentially hand you commitment or exclusivity.

- **MANAGE EXPECTATIONS**

  Phrases like, "I never heard back from my recruiter" or "X agency never briefed me on any roles" or "they never return my calls" (to name just a few), I am sure aren't too alien to you. As recruiters, we hear them all the time and they usually come from people who simply have no idea how our desks are run. It's not their fault they feel or think like that, it's our fault for not letting them know the best way of working with them post-interview.

It's important to educate candidates that the value of the recruiter-candidate relationship depends on both parties getting involved. The onus should not just lie with the recruiter. Being honest with them about the best way to deal with the partnership will manage their expectations, as long as you deliver on what you do promise them.

It's this honesty, transparency and direction that result in a respectful and long-term working partnership between you and your candidates.

It worked for me to the point that I am still in touch with many candidates today – even if I never placed them.

- **FINAL TIDBITS**
  - Referrals
  - Connect on Social Media
  - Next steps (especially if you're putting them forward for a specific role)
  - Companies they'd like to work for?
  - Exclusivity – get this for GREAT candidates only

The interview process seems like a lot when you read it but you can get all of the above information in an hour or less. The more you do it, the more you identify which areas to give deeper focus to and which you can brush over.

This technique ensures that the majority of your placements will get accepted and stronger relationships will be formed.

And just imagine, if a candidate knows how much you care about them and you take time to get to know them, when they become a client, they'll want to use you to recruit the right person for their business. And they'll know with 100% confidence that you'll only send the right candidates to them. They'll trust the advice and guidance you give, because they've experienced your service as a candidate.

A slight caveat to the above process: for freelance interviews, you will change the process to ensure you get the relevant information you need, quicker and likely over the telephone.

| INSIGHT |

You've just read the importance of conducting an in-depth interview to tighten your chances of securing placements. Just as important is the next element of **The Placement P.R.O.F.I.T. Generator™**, which is Insight; this is what you gain from your client about the vacancy that needs to be filled. And, in some way, both the **Filter** and **Insight** stages work intrinsically together.

As a recruiter, no doubt at times you will feel time pressure from the client and as a result convince yourself that you're interrupting them. So, you find yourself rushing through this part, missing cues and missing information. When in fact the truth of the matter is, the information gained here ultimately saves you and the client time later on. It also helps you have more certainty about what the client wants, which means that you will be faster at recognising it.

This leads to a win:win:win situation. It's a win for the client as you find a solution to his or her problem at a faster speed. It's a win for the candidate as the role you brief them on matches the things they want and, of course, a win for you as your results come in quicker.

| The Made-to-Match Maximiser™ |

This framework is a simple, yet effective process that ensures you cover all you need to (or at the very least focus on the areas that give you the information you need to benefit from more accurate matches   and gain you more client interviews). This will lead to more made-to-match deals.

So let's take a look at the process you should follow when finding about the client and the role.

Obtain the full **PACKAGE**.

You really need to obtain a better understanding of the client's business, their whole business. Candidates who are making a choice about their next roles want to know all they can about the company you want to send them to.

From the client's perspective, the questions you ask here show you taking an interest in their business. Understand the whole package – journey / history / values / turnover / goals, etc., whatever can help you get more insight into their business. This can all be gained within a few minutes of a call or at the start of a client meeting.

And if you're worried about the client not understanding why you need all this information, tell them why this is important and why it will make a difference in getting their ideal fit.

When you know the whole package, selling a company, regardless of size or location, becomes easier. And you start to match more than what's on the surface. You start to sell based on culture, values, and progression, in addition to skills.

If you'd don't do this level of fact-finding at the start of the process, especially with a new client, you'll end up wasting time and energy going through trial and error perhaps losing the trust of the client and the role!

POWER: One of the leading reasons why placements never amount to anything or slip away is because we haven't figured out who holds the power. And what I mean by that is, the power to actually spend money on recruitment!

How many times have you started working on a role only to find out there hasn't been official sign off?

It's not nice to be at the receiving end but some clients do engage with you to scour the market and see who is out there.

By ensuring you have sign off, you can prioritise the role. So, check in and see whether the role is one that is REAL.

PREVIOUS: In this step, you want to ask the right questions that uncover what the previous occupant of the role was like. Gain knowledge of the previous person's responsibilities, his or her background and what was it about that person that made him or her ideal for the role. Of course, the types of questions you ask will differ if the role is a new one. But just think, could you ask them who was dealing with that side of things before they decided they needed to create a new role?

Here are some key, quick-fire questions you can ask that can reveal a great plethora of information that will prove to be invaluable. This information could get you results quicker!

Now, we already know you have been chosen to recruit for your client; what if we could make you the exclusive solution, or at least the one they most trust and listen to? Would that give you the best advantage over your competitors?

You can become this by making sure you include this step in the process. Sell their **Problem** back to them before you sell them your Solution.

PROBLEM: What problems is the vacancy causing the client and why haven't they recruited someone yet?

Here you want to ask them a series of questions that will highlight what challenges they have without this person on board. What they have done so far and for how long? What hasn't worked and what challenges do they have as a result? When you present them options, you can shape the role to fit in with your candidate.

By reminding them of the challenges they face, you can be more specific about how your options can eliminate some of them. They'll thank you for it!

PROCESS: This step is vital and allows you to have complete control if done right. Here you should ask them about their recruitment process. What is it and how do they want to progress forward? Getting the minute details about who to send CVs to whilst your client is away can stop delays from occurring and prevent a post from being open for too long. It keeps momentum going for you and momentum up for your candidate who is waiting for feedback on his or her CV.

PERTINENT: This is an important part of this framework and will set you apart from your competitors. Ensure the role is an important hire for them; make sure it remains pertinent to them and is at the forefront of their priority list. This is where you gain commitment from them on interview times and dates. You want to know whether the role is as important for them as it would be for you working on it. Because if it's not, you may prioritise it further down the list to free up your time to work on roles that give you a faster ROI.

PERSUADE: Finally, once all the information is obtained from the above steps, you use it to persuade the client into your way of thinking, who you believe is the best fit, your knowledge of the market, and the urgency to see someone you recommend.

This is your chance to leverage the information gained and mold the brief as much as you can!

| TIME MANAGEMENT |

This last point of **The Placement P.R.O.F.I.T. Generator™** is one all recruiters moan about and want a miracle answer to. "I don't have enough time! How can I get some…"

Is there a miracle cure? Sadly, no and no matter how many times I teach this, unless implemented and consistently adhered to, it will always feel like time is running out.

But here's the thing: Is there a way you can stop working late into the evening? Stop taking your work home with you? Stop skipping lunch breaks simply because you're feeling overwhelmed or failing to meet looming deadlines?

The answer is YES. You see Time Management is, as the name suggests, managing your time more effectively so you work on the right things. But the truth is, you can only manage your time if you manage yourself. When you do this, it will feel like your time so you get things done without feeling stressed, burnt out, overwhelmed or losing any sign of a social life!

So, here are some techniques that can help you. And don't be surprised – you will have read and heard about them already. As I said, there is no magic wand so think of this as a more formulaic approach to help you feel time-managed.

| Arrange |

This will come as no surprise – arrange your tasks for the day into a list. Yes, that's right – a To-Do List. Here's the difference that make the difference. Construct this list the night before because when you do, whilst sleeping your unconscious starts to work on some of the elements making it easier and in more flow for you to complete them the following day. By arranging what you do on the day itself, it can often start to feel overwhelming before you've even begun.

| Analyse |

Often, people create a To-Do List and then cross off things that they have achieved. They carry forward the tasks onto the next day. Sound familiar? What you need to do is analyse the things that interrupted your day that prevented you from completing all your tasks outlined for the day.

So, if you use a To-Do List, whilst you're crossing tasks off as done, also make a note beside your list and see what distractions came in that caused you to veer off. This will come in handy in my final piece of advice at the end of this section.

| Action |

Let me ask you a question. If you had a client meeting booked into your diary, how many times would you carry that forward to another day? I'm guessing not very often, if at all.

A way to ensure you meet deadlines and don't start finding excuses for having to carry them forward onto another day is to put them in your diary just like you would an important meeting. and take action in the same way you would an important meeting. So, start using your diary, calendar, Google Calendar, Schedule app – whatever it is – add your important tasks and ensure you take action on the task.

| Assign |

Assign your tasks in order of priority.
You will be familiar with the concept I am about to explain.

| Urgent vs. Important |

Let's look at the definition of the above:
- Urgent – tasks that are required immediately
- Important – tasks that are critical to the achievement of your goals and objectives

How they work are as follows:
- URGENT tasks tend to need immediate attention; these tasks tend to act on us. They tend to be visible and insist on immediate action.

For example, the phone ringing…most cannot leave a phone ringing and to be fair, in recruitment, you definitely don't want to leave the phone ringing.

Often though, they can be mistaken for being important.

- Important – these are actions that are related to results. If something is important then it contributes to your mission / a goal / a result.

You will find yourself reacting to urgent matters often because they appear important – but on closer look, because you haven't really 'defined' what is important in your role, or, will get you the results, you'll continue responding to Urgent tasks and not the Important ones until suddenly the important ones are now time-critical and so have reached 'urgent' status – thus causing stress and overwhelm.

So, take a look at your tasks and assign them to one of four categories:

- Important
- Urgent
- Urgent and Important
- Neither urgent nor important

Some additional tips on Time Management:
1. Do one thing at a time.
2. Set time targets for each task.
3. Have a KIT KAT – as in have a break!
4. Do the things you hate first.
5. Get organized. Budget your time – that way you know how much time you have to spend elsewhere.

My final piece of advice is one that needs practice and will usually give you your time back somewhat.

6.	When necessary: **LEARN TO SAY NO.**

| TAKEAWAYS... |

- Selling is in its purest terms upserving. You have a solution that someone needs.
- Replace the word 'sell' with convince, persuade or influence.
- You will never force someone to buy something they don't want.
- Recruitment is long term – build rapport that is long lasting.
- Candidate control starts from the moment you meet them.
- Understand your candidate's real motivations – their career is in your hands.
- Pre-empt objections before they arise and handle them in part of your pitch.
- When handling objections, you simply need to add a different frame around the picture the client has given and you can create a new picture.
- Be clear what is important and what is urgent.
- Make an appointment with yourself and make sure you keep it.
- Your approach turns you into the Recruiter of Choice!

YOUR RECRUITMENT PROCESS IS DESIGNED TO DELIVER THE BEST TO YOUR CLIENT AND CANDIDATE. VIEW IT AS A PARTNERSHIP THAT CONTINUES TO ELEVATE

DEENITA PATTNI

'You can choose to come forward and shine bright or remain in the sea of sameness, where it's always a fight'.

DEENITA PATTNI

CHAPTER 7
POSITION

| **Chapter 7** - Position |

When you achieve this one aspect, the world becomes your oyster and you are followed and seen by many. You have presence and both your peers and your customer base look up to you. The better you do this, the more you're called upon to give advice, to chair panels, to be the expert voice.

When you fail to position yourself in a way that is authentic and credible, it becomes an uphill struggle. As mentioned earlier, you drift off into this 'sea of sameness' and before you know it, others are way ahead of you.

So, how can you position yourself to be the person candidates and clients want to turn to first when they have a need?

There are three elements I teach under **The Rave & Refer Radar™.**

The first is crucial in the information age we live in. Not using these tools effectively will mean you're missing out on the cream of the crop and you will fail to be seen as a thought leader. By using this strategy in the right way, you get credibility, authority and visibility in a crowded sector. What's I'm talking about here is:

ONLINE: You'll no doubt agree that we are most definitely in the digital age and as a result your clients and candidates are able to consistently stay connected to you. This means they know what you're doing, saying and thinking. I believe your online presence can be a massively effective tool for you to build rapport and be always in the front of people's minds.

And let me ask you a question that you need to honestly answer. Do you use the likes of LinkedIn or Twitter simply to advertise roles and call out for candidates? For most of you, I would imagine the answer to this is YES.

Yet what I found was by sharing thought provoking content, by engaging in groups and discussions, by blogging about trending topics, candidates and clients used to come to me of their own accord.

This separated me from all other recruiters out there and it will for you too. I believe in the mantra **Give, Give, Give, Ask!** Start thinking about how you can provide value to your connections through your online platforms and when it comes time for you to seal the deal, they'll be more than happy to reciprocate.

Let's look at it from a different viewpoint. Imagine you're a company looking to build your brand. When you think about your brand you put so much effort into building an Avatar of your ideal client including what they want, what their needs are, and what their struggles are. A company's branding is entirely reliant on what their clients want and the best brands market themselves by giving value to their clients so that when they're ready to buy, there is only one name they think of.

Yet I'm sure if you looked at your LinkedIn summary, the paragraph written would be all about you and your company and nothing about who you can help and what you can give your ideal client.

LinkedIn is the platform of choice for most recruiters when it comes to client and candidate connection. Yet the majority uses it badly, declares it a waste of time and misses out on its business benefits. What's worse, all recruiters sound the same. What sets you apart? Why should a candidate or client on LinkedIn who comes across your profile use you? It's all about positioning yourself as the go-to expert.

In my monthly 1-day implementation workshop, **LinkedIn-Cash In Converter Class™**, I have taken my clients through the fundamentals when it comes to generating qualified leads and maximizing their investment using LinkedIn. The results? More visibility, more authority and more ROI!
I believe LinkedIn is the key platform for recruiters and can make a huge difference if utilized right. As a bonus for getting this far into the book, I'd like to gift you a free eBook – 5 Essential Profile Raising Tips. Just visit: *http://clika.pe/l/7895/37259/* to download it now!

You have got to use the Internet as a marketing platform to position yourself as someone who is passionate about your industry and the people in it. Value them and they'll value you, ultimately leading to a commercial value long term.

Who could you engage with more so people know you? What knowledge and wisdom could you share with others to position you as the expert? Or will you leave your profile the same as all the average recruiters out there and fade into the background?

If you're reading this book and are this far into the content, then I doubt you will be the latter.

| WIN |

How you position yourself can make a huge difference to this next element. You see, as a recruiter you'll know that the one thing you need to do is consistently **WIN** business. Sometimes it will be informally through chatting and business development. And other times, it will be in a more formal setting – when you're pitching for a piece of business. Pitching for a piece of business is an ideal way to quadruple your earnings, as a win gives you guaranteed business and cuts out competition. So, how can you position yourself in a pitch and get that all-important WIN?

The industry has changed; more and more large corporations and businesses are formalizing their recruitment process and instead of working with any recruitment agency – they want to work with the few who are at the top of their game. And now more and more, business is won via a tendering process.

Does that make you nervous? Are you scared of standing up and presenting? Are you clueless on how to make your presentation stand out? Are you fearful of handling questions at the end in case your answer loses the business? All of these questions swirl around in your head and you hate it every time such an opportunity comes along.

So, how can you create a presentation that makes you and your organization stand out? How can you stand up with confidence and communicate your service like it's unique? It comes down to how you position not just you and your organization, but also how you position your client. It comes down to everyone's WHY!

You see, in any presentation, when you position WHY you are the right person to deal with, WHY your organization is the right one to do business with, WHY they are in the room wanting to find the best agency, you can then tell them WHY you are the best solution and WHY they need to take action now.

During my days working with an agency, my MD and I were invited to go and pitch for a client's business that we'd been recruiting for across all our teams. They were due to meet over 50 agencies over three days. And yes, you've guessed it; the slot we'd been given was on Day 3 – one before the final. If you'd been with me, you would have seen me walk into a square room, screen on the wall directly opposite a row of nine chairs where the client teams sat.

Three of us were presenting. "Oh my god. Look at their faces. They look like they've been through the mill. They look so bored!" I said to myself.

"I'd like to start off by asking you a question..."

That was all it took for them to know that this would not be a presentation reliant on words on a PowerPoint slide. Not expecting any form of interaction, they were alert and interested. And we continued to remind them why they were going through the process in the first place, outlining the problems they were likely to be faced with. We pictured what they would like their recruitment process to look like and outlined WHY we had the answer for them.

Recruiters who pitch do so by reeling out all their solutions and highlighting what their agency can do. It's all about them! That's what every recruiter does and when asked what is different about them, they ALL say the same thing.

To WIN business, you need to bring the client into the equation. And more importantly – you need to sell them the problem before you sell them your solution!

Make your presentations inspiring that clients want to buy into, not a sales pitch where clients just feel sold to!

Which brings me onto the third element...

| NETWORK |

Positioning yourself online only isn't enough. Business today operates in a Formula 1 fashion – especially recruitment. It's fast, furious and very competitive and to stay ahead, and you need to use a wide range of vehicles in order to constantly be seen and recognised. I remember my first year in recruitment; I had attended more networking events in one year than I had in my whole life.

Your network is your Net Worth

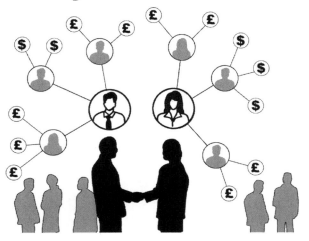

Social Media, email, blogs, and status updates are all methods that we can use to communicate with our customers/clients/candidates - sharing information, exchanging advice and liking updates. With all these digital channels available to market yourself, there seems to be a generalisation that there is no need for face-to-face anymore. WRONG!

It is just as important – if not more! People buy people and do business with people they like and have met. It's guaranteed to make your relationships stronger, build trust and last longer.

When I hired recruiters to work on my team, they seemed to prefer every single method of business developing or liaising with clients other than face-to-face, real, human interaction.

As an avid networker, at first I couldn't understand why others in the same business as me hated it. Internally, they were sociable, great communicators and had strong relations with existing clients. So, what stopped them from wanting to go out and meet people in a social setting, a technique that came so naturally to me?

Having studied human behaviour to enhance my own communication skills, I soon realised that it was their fear of rejection, the unknown and failure that stopped them from enjoying what should have been a fun and relaxing experience.

Why did I recognise it? I had been there myself and had overcome those fears.

This helped me to help others overcome whatever stopped them from enjoying the art of networking.

I believe, as effective as other tools are, in recruitment there is no substitution for face-to-face! If you're one of those people who cringes at the thought of networking, here are just a few key tips to help make your networking experiences more enjoyable:

1. **RESEARCH:** Find out who is going to be there by getting hold of an attendee list. It's a sure-fire way to feel more comfortable. Connect with those you know and let them know you'll be there. There may be a few of them who are coming on their own too and could be feeling a little apprehensive, so you'll be helping more than just yourself. You may be able to meet up with someone before the event starts and go together.

2. **READ:** How many times have you been to an event and maybe plucked up the courage to go up to a group of people only to then feel as if you have interrupted a private conversation…making you feel awkward and unwanted? The good news is, you're definitely not unwanted but yes, perhaps they weren't prepared for you yet which resulted in awkward silences and looks. Easy to avoid! You can strategically choose which groups of people to approach and which to leave until later. People's body language will tell you whether they're open to inviting you or closed for the time being. By learning how to read the room you'll never feel rejected again…

3. **RELATE:** Don't expect to walk out of networking with a handful of roles from a new client. You have to build trust by first relating to them; connect and get to know them more instead of going straight for the kill and asking for the business. Work at growing a relationship before you ask for it.

4. **RAPPORT:** Consider an opening line that is universal enough for people to find agreement or familiarity with. As the saying goes, 'the devil is in the detail' and if you start a conversation with a topic that may be controversial, then you won't necessary find rapport quickly enough. Start off with something more universally accepted.

5. **RESOURCE:** Networking can be exciting and **you're** excited to tell people about **you** and **your** services and how **you** can help them and how **you** understand the industry, how **you** do things differently and how **you** are different from others. Successful networkers are those who listen to the other person; consider what may benefit them; find out what they are looking to get out of this networking opportunity and how they could be a resource or have access to resources which could benefit them. And there is massive power in you considering who else you know that they would benefit from meeting and introducing them to each other.

6. **REFINE:** So, once you've networked and picked up/given out business cards when does networking start becoming a waste of time? When you do nothing with it once you're back in the office! So, make sure you follow up with the contacts you made. Start to refine the connection and nurture the relationship so it becomes a win:win for all.

Regardless of how fast technology advances, recruitment is an industry about people. And clients and candidates buy from people they like and trust. They can't do that if you're hiding behind a digital screen.

> **"If people like you, they'll listen to you, but if they trust you, they'll do business with you'**
>
> *ZIG ZIGLAR*

If you're a recruiter wanting to be liked, your results will remain average. Aim to be a recruiter who is TRUSTED, and you'll always win the best clients. Clients will trust you when they see the REAL you. Not if you're stuck behind a computer screen!

Later in this book, there is a separate chapter on Personal Branding by branding experts Sammy Blindell and Miles Fryer of How to Build a Brand where they'll talk more about how you position your personal brand within a company brand. It's an absolute crucial must-have for recruiters if they're to be positioned as the best in their market.

| TAKEAWAYS... |

- Visibility and Credibility will lead to Authority
- Engage on Social Media platforms – don't just use them to advertise roles
- Ensure your Client Pitch positions all of their WHYs and present with impact!
- Sell the problem before you sell the solution
- Whatever happens online must be taken offline!
- Get out there and meet clients and candidates face-to-face.
- Become the recruiter everyone wants to know and meet!
- Position yourself as the EXPERT!

If you want SUCCESS, place yourself into POSITION

DEENITA PATTNI

'LEADERSHIP IS NOT ABOUT TITLES OR POSITIONS OR FLOWCHARTS. IT IS ABOUT ONE LIFE INFLUENCING ANOTHER'.

JOHN MAXWELL

CHAPTER 8
PEOPLE

| **Chapter 8 -** People |

In recruitment, we work with the most unpredictable commodity. You can't succeed without it and at the same time, you feel they are the reason your job is tough! Whichever way you look, when challenges appear this commodity is involved!

However learn to influence in the right way and you're onto a winner. This commodity is and will continue to become your most valuable asset.

The commodity I am talking about is PEOPLE.

The skills taught in this chapter based on **The Effective Influencer™** hand you the tools to be able to influence candidates and clients externally to get the results you need by helping others reach the goals and dreams they desire. In addition, the tools have also been designed to help you internally with colleagues and managers, to create a work environment where every recruiter enjoys healthy competition whilst also working in unity together towards one goal and one mission.

There are three main groups of individuals you come into contact with throughout your career: Clients, Candidates and Colleagues. Whether you're selling jobs to candidates, candidates to clients, your services to both, or your ideas and opinions to colleagues, you must be effective at influencing them and getting the best results for all concerned.

This framework focuses on three crucial areas.

| INCREASE |

The first is without a doubt a must because without doing this, you won't have a business or a desk. Influencing your candidates in the right way will allow you to do this in the right way and give you the biggest thing you want – Choice!

I'm referring to the way in which you can **INCREASE** your candidate base. What do I mean by increase? Acquiring candidates and attracting them to you/your agency can be a task – in both a competitive market and in one that is candidate-short. There is no shortage of tools and platforms available to you where candidates are easily accessible; the challenge is influencing them and quickly enough so they choose you over your competition and stay with you over the years throughout their careers.

What many recruiters do is build their desk connecting with candidates who are actively looking. However, a study carried out by LinkedIn in 2014/5 found that 57% of UK companies recruited Passive Talent. What makes this even more interesting is that although the UK relied more heavily on recruitment agencies compared to the US, they still came up as below average when it came to approaching passive candidates! As a recruiter, are you missing out on tapping into a goldmine of talent? Are you in that below average figure?

Think about this: you walk down your high street to go to the bank. You have no intention of purchasing anything, as you don't have any need. Then you pass the shop window and your eye falls on the most beautiful outfit you have ever seen in your favourite colour. You had no plans to buy anything, remember, but it's caught your attention. You may as well try it on...doesn't mean you will buy it.

You try it on and it feels perfect. The right fit, the perfect size and it makes you feel amazing. Although you weren't in the market to buy, you buy because you know such an outfit may not be available again!

The same applies to the perfect role and so by attracting both passive and active candidates, you now have a greater chance of making placements.

Don't just go after what everyone is going after. Start to attract both those who actively want a change and those who may not have thought of moving but your opportunity compels them to. The truth is, 75% of professionals are open to hearing about new opportunities – make sure you're the one to get to them.

| INSPIRE |

You've learned in earlier chapters about how to interview candidates and uncover deep down what clients want. Here is where all of that comes together because you could absolutely have the right matches in front of you – but what's the point if you can't inspire them to consider each other?

Whether you're selling jobs to candidates or candidates to clients – you must deliver more than just the mechanics. What do I mean by that? You need to construct your pitch so they can see this person or role meeting their higher needs. meeting ultimately what they desire, meeting their WHY!

When I take my clients through **The Effective Influencer™** we use the 6 Human Needs by Tony Robbins (an adaptation of Maslow's Hierarchy of Needs) to better influence candidates and clients and turn their "no's" into "yeses."

Use the Human Needs in combination with the **Fire your D.E.S.I.R.E Dreamboard™** - a framework that shows you how to appeal to exactly what candidates and clients want when briefing them.

DREAM

EMOTION

SUCCESS

INTEREST

REASON

ECONOMIC

Fire Their
D.E.S.I.R.E
Dreamboard™

I remember when I signed up with a recruitment agency because I was interested in Trainer opportunities. One recruiter, who worked at REED, a well-established agency in the UK, emailed me a role expecting me to say yes. From the document she sent me, the role looked completely different from what I wanted in terms of the sector; it did not seem to match my market experience and I couldn't see how this would help me reach my bigger aim. Now, I was open enough to at least explore more about it and so attempted to call and email her suggesting we have a chat.

This never happened! She never replied back to me, never called me, and never let me know the outcome.

Now, although there was a whole host of things she did wrong there, let's just focus on the area we're discussing in this point. If she had called and influenced me by explaining how the role met those higher needs, how the role matched what I was ultimately looking to achieve – even if it wasn't perfect, I may have considered it.

Truth is, all candidates aren't like me. In the above scenario, I still attempted to find out more. However, if you act like the recruiter above, most candidates would have rejected even considering the role. And you would be classed as a recruiter who *'has no idea what I want and always briefs me on the wrong roles.'*

Next time, inspire your clients and candidates. Influence them in a way that reaches them inside. Otherwise you may find you lose out when you could've had the placement in the palm of your hand!

| INTEGRATE |

The majority of this book focuses on you, your clients and candidates. However, there is one group of people with whom you spend a vast majority of time and it's imperative to be influential around them too. I'm talking about your work colleagues – peers and managers.

You must learn to **INTEGRATE** yourself in a manner where you're able to have a positive influence during conflicts, opinions and ideas. Working in a sales environment breeds competition and what starts out as healthy competition can easily turn into resentment. Don't get me wrong. It's good to have your own opinions and ideas and you don't have to agree with everything someone else says. But how you influence situations can make a huge difference and if done the right way, you can find agreement and a way forward using a collaborative approach.

| How? |

By always keeping in mind the bigger picture. You see, when you stay focused on in the details, you will tend to find disagreement. When you take a step back and think about the bigger picture and think about what it is you both are trying to achieve, you'll eventually realize that you actually want to achieve the same thing. And when you start to communicate at this higher level, you will integrate better and with both sets of opinions and ideas taken into consideration; you'll find a way forward that works for both.

| Teamwork |

Not just in recruitment, but in any professional working environment, you're required to work in a team. When the team gels together, magic happens. Then someone new joins and the boat has been rocked slightly. You want to avoid this boat going into stormy seas!

In The Effective Influencer™, we take a look at three key techniques to enhance team integration and one of them is Dr. Bruce Tuckman's Team Development Model.

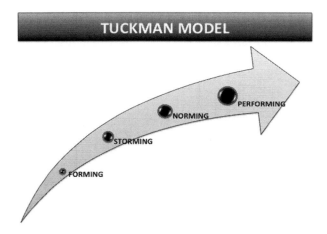

When someone joins a team, it's daunting for both the person coming into it and the people already existing.

The person coming in has to prove him or herself may be nervous, want to settle in quickly and feel part of it.
Existing team members may feel threatened, worry about having to pass clients over or about whether this person will cause conflict and whether they will be given more attention from management.

Those are just a few thoughts that may be going through your head. The great news is Bruce Tuckman states this is normal. And even if you have been part of a team for a long time, you will experience the four stages of the Tuckman Model every time a new member joins or a restructure occurs. Here are his four stages:

Forming: The first stage is when new teams are formed, come together or a new person joins. This is where team members are positive and polite. This stage brings a little anxiety as people are not sure what the new person brings to the team yet – but are excited enough. This stage can last for a while as everyone makes an effort with the new person. The new person is also anxious as his or her role is unclear. They want to integrate well into the team and so make an effort to get to know their colleagues. This can almost be the observation stage where everyone is observing each other and making every effort not to be judged.

Storming: This is where team members begin to form opinions and voice them. Because boundaries are pushed, this is the stage where cliques may start to form and conflicts begin. Different working styles can cause problems and this can be frustrating for the team as a whole. If not careful, this is where teams can fail and performances or results start to fall. Storming can also escalate if assumptions are made. Managers can make decisions based on their own aim and can elevate a new team member's status unknowingly causing jealousy and conflict within the team. Authority could be challenged.

If you can get past this stage, you will move over to…

Norming: This is where team colleagues begin to find mutual respect for each other's opinions and appreciate each other's strengths. Differences highlighted in Storming start to get resolved and things start to become normal. They know each other better and even start to socialize together more having drinks after work or lunch. They support each other both professionally and personally. You can jump from this stage back to Storming at times – especially when new tasks come into play or managers make decisions – only you're better at returning to norming. This then leads to…

Performing: The team works as one! They perform for the bigger goal and work cohesively together. Everyone feels part of the team and this also helps the manager to delegate and develop teams.

Once you understand this model, you can recognise the signs and act on them. Once combined with the other strategies I teach here, you can integrate better with your colleagues and manager and work towards achieving big results for longer!

Teamwork Makes the Dream Work

| TAKEAWAYS... |

- Go for candidates that your competition isn't looking at.
- Approach passive candidates consistently – they're interested and could well be interested in what you have to offer.
- Build your candidate base even when you don't have roles for them.
- Inspire your clients and candidates and appeal to their big picture outcome. The no's will turn into yeses!
- You are not alone – work with your colleagues and managers not against them.
- You can move mountains by being influential – this in turn will influence without you even realising or asking.

Influence is our Inner Ability to lift PEOPLE up to our perspectives

JOSEPH WONG

'Get closer than ever to your Customers.
So close that you tell them what they need well before they realize it themselves'.

STEVE JOBS

CHAPTER 9
PROSPECTS

| **Chapter 9 -** Prospects |

One of your most prized assets and one that will either make or break you and that is your prospects, commonly known as your client base!

What many recruiters fail to do when they work in the industry is see their desk as a mini-business. In recruitment, more than any other industry, your entrepreneurial spirit is one that you need to tap into. This is what will make you great! You must treat your desk as a mini commercial entity that operates under a larger umbrella.

Just as a business creates a strategy to attract clients, to research their markets, to build on trends, to innovate, to profit and to build – you must also do the same for your specific desk. Even if you are one in a team of three, you must strategise your desk to get results that fit into the wider team and agency business.

Failing to strategise and view your desk as a business will have you reaching out for everything and anything. You'll end up chasing business that has very little return, competing with too many other recruiters for the same job and having lots of one-hit wonders. Every time you business develop, it will feel like you're starting from square one and that will begin to weigh heavily. This can have a whole host of effects from self-doubt, and a break down in confidence, to resentment and exiting the industry.

When I teach my clients the three techniques within the **A.I.M. to Claim Principle™** they enjoy developing their businesses because they know exactly what to do, who to go after and where opportunities lay – working smarter not harder and reaping the RESULTS!

| **Where are you right now?** |

When you forget to do this first step, you can find yourself all over the place with no idea of what you have at your fingertips. By ensuring this part is carried out whether you're starting a new desk or inheriting one, you spend time wisely and can see the opportunities easily. This first step is to **ASSESS**; assess where you are right now.

| Where next? |

So, you've assessed your client base and now this second step gets you out there and exploring. Even if you're already an expert in your field, start to INVESTIGATE more about your market.

What are the best resources you should be part of or get involved with? What could you be reading that would give you the best insight into your market? Who do you know already whom you can reach out to and meet? Because you don't just need to be the expert in your field, you need to use this expertise to get you in front of clients more quickly so you can start claiming the work as your own.

| How? |

Once you've assessed and investigated, now you can plan an actionable strategy. You take all this information and **MAP** your market.

What do I mean by MAP? Well, with all the assessing and investigating, you want to implement a way of working whereby you have choice all around, a choice of roles with which to brief to your candidates, a choice of candidates to bring to your clients and a choice of offers to present to your candidates.

Today, recruiters work on one candidate at a time, one role at a time, one offer at a time. What if you were able to send your candidate to not just one role, but instead three? What if you had a larger share of the market? You could present candidates with three different offers so you never lose that candidate to another agency. You could present more than one candidate to a job because you have a larger share of the candidate market.

That would have you working smarter and being the number one recruiter because you have the share of the market!

One familiar way of doing this is to conduct a SWOT analysis:

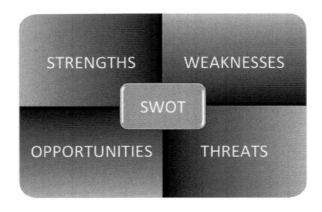

Most people who conduct a SWOT Analysis base their findings on all external factors. However, to be able to MAP your market successfully and align it with your agency's offering means you must focus on the areas where you and your agency are strong and improve to work on those elements that can help grow and develop you as a recruiter as well as the overall business. This will allow you to work successfully regardless of future economic factors that may affect your market and industry. When you MAP your market using a SWOT analysis, it allows you to pre-empt any surprises that could stop you from achieving your goals.

Strengths and weaknesses relate to internal factors, while opportunities and threats cover external ones.

Strengths – What does the agency do well?
Weaknesses – What may prevent goals and objectives from being achieved?
Opportunities – What opportunities are available to improve productivity or growth?
Threats – What conditions could damage businesses performance?

Below are just some questions you should consider when undertaking a SWOT Analysis:

| STRENGTHS |

What are your personal strengths?
What does the company do well?

What do you do well?
What is the good track record?
What do other people see as your strengths?
Where does the organisation compete well?

| WEAKNESSES |

What can be developed?
What could you improve?
What is working less optimally than you wish?
What is being done badly?
What is the competition doing better?
What should you avoid doing?

| OPPORTUNITIES |

If there were no constraints, what would you like to do?
What might be possible?
What will happen in the next few years?
Where do you/your organisation want to be in five years' time?
Who might you want to work with?
What could be a win–win situation?
How may new technologies change your practices?
What financial/governmental/legislative changes can benefit you in the near future?

| THREATS |

What are the barriers to you or your market's development?
What sort of obstacles do you face?
Who else might move in and take over your tasks/job/business?
What are rival organisations doing?
Can you fund the short and long term?
Will new technologies/developments change the way you do things?
What change is coming?

When you perform the above along with the other techniques taught in this module, you will create a strategy that will keep you on **TASK**, on **TIME** and on **TARGET**.

| TAKEAWAYS... |

- View your desk as a mini business.
- Create a strategy that gives you a better return on your investment.
- Allow your strategy to give you a bigger share of the pool, making you the expert within it.
- Align your strategy with that of your organisation; work together on gaining market share.
- Become knowledge about your area and create key accounts.
- Get more from less.

If you don't AIM for the best prospects, you're likely to do business with any prospect.

TODD DUNCAN

CHAPTER 10
GUEST
CHAPTERS

'LEADERSHIP IS ABOUT UNLOCKING PEOPLE'S POTENTIAL TO BECOME BETTER'.

BILL BRADLEY

| **Chapter 10 -** Guest Chapters |

| **The Manager's Perspective** |

Mike Berry, Country Manager, Aquent/Vitamin T
www.aquent.com

Throughout my career as a recruiter, I was fortunate to have some amazing managers. There were also a couple that left a lot to be desired. But in the way you do in life, you learn from both positive and negative experiences and you ensure you take the best bits, develop them, share them and build on them.

My manager, before I embarked on my entrepreneurial journey, was a gentleman by the name of Mike Berry. When he took over the role of MD, I had already been managing teams. I was always keen to inspire and help others achieve great results and realize their potential. Now, Mike didn't just work with me to develop my managerial skills, he also earned my respect in many different ways. His approach not only allowed me to grow and be expressive with ideas and strategies, but also, at the same time equipped me with the ability to understand his objectives for the business. This meant that we worked as a team. I knew how to work with him so that he got what he needed and in turn he gave me the leadership I needed to flourish. It made me an inspiring leader as well as a savvy businessperson. And I am sure it gave Mike a follower he could inspire.

'Be the kind of leader you would follow'

In this first Guest Chapter, Mike Berry gives you his perspective – The Manager's Perspective. This will provide you with sound and solid advice if you're a manager or planning on taking on a managerial role. It will give you insight on how managers view their teams, so that you can find the best way of working with your manager so you achieve more together.

| **A Manager's role** |

People often ask me what makes a good manager. After all, some managers make it look really easy and others seem to be continually fighting to understand what is going on in their world.

What can a manager do to be as effective as possible and what are the most important things to remember?

Here are a few thoughts:

| 'Big Picture' view |

As a manager and leader you need to have the ability to see the whole business even if you're only managing part of it. Where do **you** and **your** team fit in? How can you take what you know and create a team-focused vision and plan that adds the most value to the whole? If you don't, who else will?

Having this understanding at the core at all times will mean it's at the forefront of everything you do and every decision you make. Ultimately, that's how what you do will enable you to get where you need to be.

Because the truth is, (that many managers fail to acknowledge), how can you possibly expect your team to be as good as they can be if they haven't got the big picture either?

As a manager, your job is to paint the big picture. Just because you know where you are going doesn't mean everyone else does. You need to tell and show the team where you are trying to go. You should be able to articulate the steps you will take as a business and, most importantly, make it **relevant** to the individuals.

Too many businesses have objectives that are communicated amongst the managers and owners but not communicated down to those that are key to the business – the recruiters. When they buy into the vision you have as a manager or owner, you attract loyal and committed staff that see the business as their own.

Create milestones and checkpoints so the team knows where they stand. This alone is not enough. Your people also need to understand the WHY! You need to be able to tell the story and show the way. Tell the story in a way that engages everyone. Stories bring people in, so learn to tell them well. And don't just do it once and expect everyone to get it. Keep revisiting the vision/goal, the company's WHY. and ensure people know where the business is.

Now, like any business, sometimes goals and targets set at the start may lag behind. Don't sugarcoat this; be transparent with your team because if the business/team is behind the goal/target, the only way to get results back on track is if they know the plan and the path forward.

They feel engaged, included and inspired because they become part of the solution and are not seen as the problem. And during these times, find the positives in the progress made and communicate them effectively!

| Lead the business |

Now, do not be mistaken! As a manager, you're being watched all the time, by everyone, by your boss, your peers and your team.

As a manager, especially in recruitment, you have to lead by example. Everybody looks for a leader and your team needs to see you working towards the goal. If you're expecting them to do so, then you've also got to show evidence of this. When you lead, you have followers and therefore your approach, behaviour and communication style will ultimately determine the approach, behaviour and communication style that your team takes.

| Coach future managers |

Great managers breed great managers. And when you see members of your team become inspiring leaders, you know you've done something right. And if your recruitment business is to grow, like many are today, you need to develop and grow as a manager too. As a manager, if you have any aspiration to grow and take on more responsibility, but without undoing all the work you have put into the team, then you need to make sure others will take up the challenge of managing and leading.

So don't be territorial; always look to bring people up in the business. A growing business can't survive with just you managing/leading. Identify the next generation of managers and mentor them; work with them to make sure they have the skills and desire necessary to grow themselves.

| Hire the best person for the job |

As a manager, you need to recognize great talent for the business. This means you need to work out what the job role you have available is now and what it will develop into in the future. Don't expect a fully formed expert. Be realistic in your wish list. Take their desire to succeed and their ability to learn as strong indicators of a great hire.

When promoting internally, use the same criteria. People should not be promoted just because they've been there the longest. Their characteristics, skills, desire and approach still need to be taken into account.

| Get out of the way |

If you want the team to grow and take the pressure off you, get out of the way of their development. Good people need space to grow and learn and, at times, make mistakes. Let them. After all, there is no failure, only feedback. You cannot grow a business if everything stops with you. You are not perfect and thinking so could be your biggest downfall. Don't try and do it all for them. You need to be a mentor for them without suffocating them. You can stifle great people if you look over their shoulders every day. How can they come up with new ideas and approaches if you don't give them the space to do so?

As a manager, you won't always have the answer to everything and that's OK. You can learn as much from your subordinates as they can learn from you. Trust them and learn from everyone you talk to. Which makes the next point even more imperative…

| Listen to your team |

They know things you don't. As you grow as a manager you will lose sight of some of the day-to-day things your team does. It's OK to let that happen. Allow people to be experts and add value individually.

| A recruiter's role |

As a recruiter, it's important to create a lasting and winning relationship with your manager. In too many recruitment businesses, you hear of how the team of recruiters either doesn't like, can't work with, or doesn't respect the manager. Why? What stops the two from finding that win-win situation where they work together to meet both company and individual objectives?

As a recruiter, do the same as your manager! By this I mean, understand your role in the business and consider how what you do affects everyone around you and impacts the overall performance and direction.

You should have an understanding of the vision and goals, an appreciation of what your team is expected to do and how you can improve things. Be a leader within your team, even if it's just you. Recognise and appreciate that others may be experts where you're not and consider this an advantage, not a weakness. Use each other's strengths to succeed and get the best for both you as an individual (after all, you do work in sales) and the team.

Here are a few things to focus on:

| Listen |

Listen to both your managers and peers; it doesn't mean you need to hide your opinions or thoughts on matters. But really listen by being open to a different perspective. Having your head down and being oblivious to everything around you often damages the business over time. Listening to what others are talking about in their day-to-day activities will help you focus on the right areas and transform you into a valuable resource.

| Question |

Ask questions of everybody, especially your manager and peers. You know you're a great listener when you have questions about what you hear. Here's something interesting you may want to note: when you're not really listening, it's because you're too busy inside your head convincing yourself that you're right. That's when you miss the opportunity to ask questions and learn more. Make sure you ask so you get a better picture. This will help you put your efforts in the right direction and improve your effectiveness. Don't accept blindly. Use your knowledge to question.

| Take Charge |

Take responsibility for your own development, your own desk and your own activities. Don't wait to be told what to do. Make sure you understand your role and your own responsibilities so that you can be proactive and be seen to add value. It's your job. Own it.

| Open and Honest |

Be grown up. Don't lie (about anything). There is no point trying to fool yourself and others. It will nearly always get found out and you will suffer in the long term. Be open and honest especially with your manager; they deserve this and will support you through anything when they don't feel you're hiding something. How can they help if you can't be straight with them? This is the key to building a great relationship with your manager, which is long lasting and mutually respectful!

Let's face it, recruiters have a bad enough reputation as it is, so don't add to it by trying to "pull a fast one" with colleagues, clients or candidates. Having such a reputation is a sure way of stalling your career and in the information/digital age we live and work in now, it won't take long before you're found out

If you don't know, ask, don't bulls**t. In my experience, you generally get exposed if you try to pretend to have experience/knowledge that you don't. The result is that you appear unreliable and unhelpful. These are not good things to be known for if you want to progress.

If you haven't done something that was expected of you or you know you're not going to meet expectations, raise your hand and admit it. Get it out in the open and deal with it because the reality is, you're more likely to find a solution together. Managers value this approach and will help work things out.

| Team Approach |

Recognise the value of a TEAM. The best performers use their teams to help. Working together, you are so much stronger and can achieve more, faster. Make sure you know how good your colleagues are and play to their strengths and yours. Many hands make your job easier so don't try and fight everybody.

| Aim high |

Challenge yourself. Push yourself to learn more, do more, and exceed expectations both internally and externally. Challenge your peers to have an equally strong belief in delivering great service and results. Everyone is working from the same page and the same values.

| What a Manager looks for |

As a manager, I always look for someone about whom I know the rest of the team will say, *"I am so glad you are on my team because you bring something that makes us all better/stronger."* This is a critical factor and leads to the creation of a really good strong team that will overachieve as a group.

So, if you want to be noticed by your manager and want to build that mutually respectful relationship, show your manager the key skills: a really good attitude, intelligence and curiosity, willingness to learn, and confidence (as you have to be able to hold your own). Be open-minded and be a great listener. I always look for honesty and evidence of ethical working, self-managing and self-motivating make a great team member because a manager can reduce the micromanagement element, giving people the space they need to succeed. Above all you need to be a fantastic communicator to your manager, your peers and your external contacts.

As a recruiter, if you're ever at your desk wondering what your manager has on his mind, here's something to have awareness around: Knowing these golden nuggets that are about to follow will help you to see the manager's perspective and allow you to change your approach so you can be the kind of recruiter who adds value and is seen as a valuable asset!

Managers are constantly under pressure about not only inspiring the team they lead but also meeting overall company objectives.

Once I have a vision and a plan, I then think about how to bring the team with me. That's what great managers do in every recruitment business. They constantly have a number of questions going on inside their heads.

What will the business look like in a year/two years/five years? Will changes externally mean the need to change focus and direction?

How will this affect the team? How can I get the team motivated and enthusiastic? What do they need? How do they want to be motivated? Is there anyone in the team that can act as an advocate and help make change work? Who is showing potential to grow and take on more responsibility? Does that help the business and them move forward? What can I do differently to make things even better?

As managers, if we don't spend time out of the day-to-day operations, how will we know that the direction we are taking is the one that will give the best result? That's why as managers, our decisions can sometimes seem to come out of thin air and cause mistrust but in fact are made after a lot of thought. And that's why having a team that has some of the traits discussed in this chapter is key.

'YOU CAN HAVE ANYTHING
YOU WANT
IF YOU
DRESS FOR IT'.

EDITH WARD

| **Dressed to Impress!** - Jo Smallbones

As recruiters, part of our role is to let our candidates know the best dress code for their interviews. Your candidate will have let you know what their ideal environment is when it comes to their career place. So, if your candidate is off to interview at a corporate-feel office all suited and booted, and they're more of a dress down type of person, you're already off to disastrous start! They're already feeling uncomfortable which has affected their state, and if you remember from earlier in the book, that affects their behavior – and this will affect not only their results, but also yours!

How you dress has a direct impact on your emotional state that can have an effect on your performance. That is true for you as a recruiter, too! Whether or not you're a suit person, you want to dress with confidence so it gives you confidence internally that then transpires externally.

Jo Smallbones helps her clients achieve career and business success by transforming their wardrobes from self-critical to self-confident turning stale to style. Jo found herself feeling uninspired, stuck for ideas and bored with her clothing choices. This resulted in low self-esteem and little self-belief that led to fading into the background with her clients, friends and family. Today, as an Image Consultant, Jo helps clients discover how they feel from what they wear so that your style best represents the real, authentic you so you can be yourself when in front of your clients and candidates. This will ultimately help you achieve and maximize your full potential.

In this chapter, Jo shares with you some golden nuggets on how create your STYLE CONFIDENCE.

How to "wear" your individuality and achieve career/business success

When it comes to dressing for business I have a holistic approach.

I believe that clothes are not about putting on a costume and pretending, unless you're an actor. They are not to be used as a tool for hiding behind and looking like everyone else – that's a uniform.

Clothes should be used to reflect who you truly are and should make you feel positive, confident and comfortable with your personality and character. Dressing congruently with your mood, inner beliefs and personality gives you individuality and most importantly self-confidence in any situation.

Now as you read this, you may be already questioning whether your personal dress sense won't fit in with work! Absolutely, and it's no easy task to combine authentic dressing with keeping it appropriate for the workplace. Dressing for your truth opens up a whole array of choices and options, which means there's a lot more scope for getting it wrong for the workplace. This is why the boring universal grey suit/dress becomes the easier option when deciding what to wear and why so many people resort to it. That's where they go wrong!

Be honest; is your personality boring, unimaginative and dull? That is what a grey, off-the-peg suit can sometimes reflect. I would guess not - which is you want to learn how to combine your authentic dressing with workplace appropriateness.

In doing so, you'll achieve a business look that sets you apart from the others and still have an edge in today's competitive business environment.

| First Impressions |

Let's address this tricky subject because very often I get two polar opposite reactions.

The first is that prickly comment, "I never judge a book by its cover."

When taken literally, this is not really a good metaphor because any good publisher will ensure the book has an eye-catching cover so it stands out on the bookshelf to tempt its potential reader into buying it.

Now the truth is, you might not want to every day, but when in front of your clients and candidates, both in person and over the phone, standing out amongst your competitors is crucial for success. First impressions need not be seen as judgmental; they are a gut instinct our sub-conscious mind controls. There is a certain level of assessment based on what you see before you, even if you are not consciously aware you are doing it.

The second and the more contentious is when people discriminate and judge based on colour, gender, age, disability and size. Unfortunately, this is the one that taints the expression "first Impressions" – even though it's only a small-minded minority of people who judge to this extreme.

Thankfully the majority sees 'first impressions' as a way to **communicate** and they acknowledge that getting it right is more relevant and important today than it has ever been.

We live in a speedy world of convenience where we are looking for an instant connection with the people we work with. In recruitment, your clients and candidates are looking for recruiters who they like and can easily relate to, recruiters who are positive and self-confident who come across as honest. This can be impossible to communicate in just a few seconds and so it makes sense to use your image as visual shorthand to speedily express who you are, your talents and your abilities, as you will find your target market will connect easier with you and get what you're about.

Spending time to master dressing for your individuality whilst keeping within the businesses boundaries of appropriateness is a life skill that's worth learning especially as it's going to benefit your business and career success.

Here are my key tips and points to help you successfully combine your individuality with workplace appropriateness:

| APPEARANCE |

Think of the best two or three key words that describe you in your business role. If you find this challenging, ask a friend or colleague who knows you well. When you have deciphered these key words, try to reflect them in your appearance. For example, meticulous and organized can be projected in a look that is classically neat with very little fuss, therefore avoid patterns or too much jewelry. Clean, simple lines work best (but avoid looking staid and dated).

If you are friendly, fun, and a motivating supportive manager, a navy suit or dress would cover the professional aspect the managerial role requires but you still need to get across your friendly approachable character. Consider accessorizing with a tie, necklace or scarf/cardigan in a cheery colour that suits you.

Do not fall into the trap of "fun" comedy ties, "cute" jewelry or bold patterns to reflect your fun side; you could be going over the appropriate boundary. An accessory in a plain colour or subtle pattern that suits your colouring, face shape and flatters your body shape is enough to express the sunnier side of your personality.

| ALIGN |

Smart Casual is the one dress code that everyone interprets in their own way, but very few realise what it entails. For women it means replacing the jacket with knitwear, for men it's losing the tie and/or replacing a suit jacket with a coordinating moleskin or tweed "sports" jacket. Jeans do not fit into smart casual, nor do maxi dresses, tunics or leggings.

Appropriate dress codes depend on the businesses practical requirements and its culture, and every business will have different rules on what's required. As a general guide, think about what your customers or clients and work colleagues expect.

When visiting a client, research what their staff/managers are wearing and ensure you wear items that are congruent with your business, yet still fit in with the corporate image of the business.

For example, if it's a traditional, conventional business, wear a trouser/skirt suit and tie (men) and make sure you are immaculately groomed, from head to toe. To avoid disappearing into the sea of grey-suited candidates your tie, shirt, lining in your jacket and the small details such as your watch, belt and shoes should tone and coordinate – no clashing of patterns and colours. Women can wear coordinating jewelry, but ensure it's subtle enough to compliment the outfit rather than scream "look at me" – a definite image breaker is jangly jewelry.

For a young innovative business, where the staff dresses more casually, avoid falling into the trap of denim jeans. The business may have a more casual approach to business wear, however if you're on a client visit, then as a mark of respect, dress up, otherwise it can be seen as bad manners and you have not made an effort. When I advise to dress up I don't necessarily mean wear a suit as this may not fit in with a younger, dynamic innovative business. For example, when you visit a marketing/advertising or media environment being more creative would fit in well and show your client that you're aligned with their business and therefore a perfect representative.

Plus you'll also feel at home which means you'll perform with confidence and instill confidence in your client. Consider wearing something that's on trend – caution with this if you're older - wearing more colour could be an alternative option.

As recruiters, the key thing is dressing to reflect you whilst fitting in with the business culture and the options are limitless. Getting professional advice from a personal stylist who can creatively put together an individual look that expresses you whilst remaining within the business dress codes and culture of your client is worth investing in. There are so many anomalies that could result in getting it very wrong and in a client meeting you may only get one bite at the cherry. So, is it really worth taking that risk?

| APPRORIATE |

Too much flesh is a distraction! Remember that short skirts ride up even higher when one sits down. If it clings, creases and is see-through, wrap your sandwiches in it! It's a sure-fire way to get noticed, but do you want to be noticed for all the wrong reasons?

For men, a suit that rides up the arms and pulls across the shoulders or leaves sagging material around the back of the legs because it's too big is not a good look. Buttons stretching to their maximum hold and exposing flesh isn't a great look either, so practice sitting down to check for gaping buttons and baggy bottoms.

| ALTERNATIVES |

I know it's the easy option, but black is what everyone else will be wearing, if not black then charcoal grey and you want to be remembered. Navy is a good alternative to black and an easier colour to wear.

You may still want to wear black or grey as your base colour in your outfit but avoid looking like a dreary dark day by injecting a "splash" of colour. Colours are a fantastic mood enhancer and you will find wearing some colour will brighten and lift your mood and the mood of those around you. That's a massive bonus for a recruiter!

When you wear a colour that suits you, your eyes sparkle, you will miraculously lose the dark circles and lines that give away your tiredness and stress levels and you will project self- confidence.

| ATTRIBUTE |

By attribute I mean use your clothes to reflect your character, charm and spirit but keep within your instinct boundaries of knowing whether or not you can pull it off. It's a fine line between playing it too safe and going over the top. Knowing exactly what works for you gives you the confidence to step outside your comfort zone and try something new. Have fun and enjoy your wardrobe.

| AUTHENTIC |

Reflecting your true self in your appearance and being more aware of the non-verbal messages you are transmitting helps you communicate more effectively. Be authentic. Whilst something may look good on your friend or work colleague, it may not be suitable for you. Go with your gut instinct otherwise it ends up being an expensive mistake sat on a pile of other unworn items in your wardrobe. Style is not about being good looking, having a fabulous figure or having lots of money, it is about confidently stepping forward and saying

'This is me and I love being me!'

For her latest video blogs, packed full of style tips and to sign up for her **FREE *"Today I feel like wearing..."*** series of videos designed to help you dress for your mood. Visit her website: ***www.josmallbones.co.uk***

'Your Brand is What Other People Say About you When you're Not in the Room'.

JEFF BEZOS, CEO, AMAZON

This next guest chapter is crucial for you whether you're a business owner, a solo entrepreneur, recruiter or a recruiter employed by an agency.

As a recruitment business owner/solo entrepreneur, it's imperative to understand what your brand is attracting and repelling. Too many times, as we start our businesses, we fail to give our business brand the attention it needs and there is a strong misalignment between what you stand for and believe in and what your brand says. This often leads to lost business without realising why. In addition, this lack in clarity can often mean hiring the wrong recruitment staff for your agency!

As a recruiter working within an agency, the content in this chapter will give you a distinct advantage in supporting your agency and in getting your marketing and strategy right so it reflects your personal brand – you can become a magnet, attracting the perfect client!

Advice and value supplied by these next two authors, if taken into serious consideration, will transform the way you look at your business and the results you start to get.

| How To Build A Strong Brand In Recruitment |

Written by Sammy Blindell, CEO at *www.*
HowToBuildABrand.org *and author of the award winning book, 'How To Build A Brand – The 7 Reasons Why Customers DON'T Choose You'*

There are five fundamental principles you need to follow when building a strong personal and business brand for yourself. These principles apply across all sectors, especially in recruitment, where there is an emotional transaction as well as a physical and financial one. In this chapter, we're going to cover the basics of these principles. They are:

1. Belief
2. Research
3. Association
4. Nurturing
5. Domination

| Let's start with BELIEF... |

Think of the last time you spent money on something BIG and you had to make a decision between two providers. Maybe it was a sofa, something for you personally, or perhaps it was your first vehicle. The "thing" you were purchasing was similar in price, value and availability at both stores. You had never spent money with either company before and this was an amount of money that was significant to you.

What was it that tipped you over the edge to choose from one and not the other? When it really came down to it, if they were so similar, what was it that pushed you over the tipping point to spend your money with the one you chose?

In our 21 years of creating, building and expanding brands across all sectors (including recruitment), the answer to this question comes down to two things: credibility and trust. The two feed off one another to create a marriage that turns strangers into friends and friends into lifetime customers. Without these two key components being built into the DNA of your personal and business brand, you will never have a brand. Oh, and by the way, there's a reason why three out of five of the letters in the word **BRAND** are **DNA** – your brand is the life support system behind everything your business says, does and delivers.

You see, people don't even give away their email address for free anymore. They would rather spend money than give you their personal data! So, getting them to trust you is a significant achievement, especially in the recruitment industry, where people are buying people as opposed to products. But how do you build trust in a heartbeat? How can you create a rapport between your ideal customers and your personal brand that is so strong that they feel immediately connected and bonded to it? The first step is **CONSISTENCY**.

Consistency builds trust, trust builds credibility, and credibility builds your personal brand. If your brand is inconsistent, people will believe that what you deliver will be inconsistent too. An inconsistent personal brand that is then layered with inconsistent messages, inconsistent colours, inconsistent marketing materials and inconsistent quality is highly confusing.

| People do not buy in a state of confusion |

Obvious, right? So why is it then that we see inconsistency so often? Here's a very common example that we see with inconsistent recruitment brands all the time:

- Someone from the company goes to a business event. They say great things about what their recruitment business does. They go on a bit as they haven't really nailed their pitch yet, but what they said sounds impressive enough. They now have a good personal brand in your opinion. You don't trust them fully, but you don't distrust them, because you don't really know them yet.

- They give you their business card and it doesn't come across in the same way that the person did. Hmm… They talked about quality, but their business card doesn't give you the same feeling. What does that logo even mean to me? It looks like they created something that looks nice, but isn't attractive to me as the customer. The visual representation of the business just doesn't give you the same feelings you had when you met them in person. Trust has now halved by this point.

- You get back to the office and go to the website address on their card. Hmm… again. It doesn't even look the same. Is this the right company? You search around, but they don't appear anywhere else, or you find other results about them that aren't positioning them very well. It must be them, but you've given up caring. Trust is down to about 2% from the 80% it started off at.

- What they said at the beginning sounded really interesting. How disappointing that they couldn't back it up. But they highlighted a gap in my business and now I'm interested in what they were selling. But I can't be bothered to search for them anymore. I'm going to look for it elsewhere.

What a waste. You spent your time, energy and money getting them to understand what they need and why they need it from YOU, only to push them to go and find it somewhere else. That's BRANDALISM!

Let's be clear here… your competitors are seeking more and more influential and effective ways to impact upon your prospects and customers to build their reputation over yours. Don't give them any opportunity to overcharge and under-deliver on the promises they have made to YOUR ideal customers, because you may never get the chance to put it right.

You KNOW you are the best company to help them, so it's not just your right to claim leadership in your industry, it's your duty.

Don't let your ideal customers down because you only did what was necessary. Go the extra mile to do what is right and get your strategy in place now – before you continue to go out into the world and create a loose cannon approach to attracting customers. This is a very time consuming, energy zapping, expensive and ineffective way to grow your business. Investing in creating and building your personal brand (notice we say "brand" and not "branding," which is the logo element) now will ensure that while your competitors are running around like headless chickens (focusing on money rather than the customer experience), you will be winning the right customers in the right places, in the right way, at the right times. You'll attract the money naturally by building your personal brand and not your bank balance. This is by far the most effective, productive and cost effective way to grow your business and cut your marketing expenses dramatically – letting your customers do the work of building your reputation (and therefore your bank balance) for you.

Let's put this into perspective... On an average day, you are exposed to an excess of 60,000 brands from the moment you wake up to the moment you go to sleep. So are your ideal customers! How you make a first, last and lasting impact on them is vital if you want to ensure that you and your brand reputation are number one on their minds when they need what you provide. And when they do find you online, you need to ensure they don't just bounce straight onto somewhere else, because you didn't invest correctly in your own key messaging to ensure the trust was there.

Your brand positioning will determine whether your prospects pick up the phone to you or someone you compete with. This is especially true of the recruitment industry, where it is perceived (incorrectly) that what you do is dispensable. So, the best way you can ensure you have the leading edge on your competitors is to strengthen your personal brand by creating massive and immediate rapport. You can do this by implementing a solid brand communications strategy to not just win your customers, but to create a lifetime relationship with them that keeps paying. This then needs to be rolled out across all of your customer facing touch-points and all the places that your ideal customers are hanging out in the highest concentration. Your strategy must build immediate trust, credibility and BELIEF. Your personal brand is the first connection a prospect has with your recruitment company. It's the reputation you have built and all the things that other people say about you when you aren't there.

If they trust your brand, what you stand for and the messages behind it, they'll take the next steps with YOU to find out more.

How you position yourself and your personal reputation is critical to start building trust in the first place and it starts with being able to clearly articulate 'what one single message tells your customer all about you?' It must be clear to them within 3-7 seconds why they should care that you even exist, or they're going to bounce straight onto another company. If you'd like some help in creating an articulate, compelling and engaging answer to this question, download this free chapter from our book at: ***https://howtobuildabrand.org/7-reasons-why-customers-dont-choose-you-free-chapter/***

| Let's move onto the RESEARCH... |

According to Forbes online magazine, statistics show that 8 out of every 10 businesses fail in their first year. This is a much higher statistic than it was only two years ago, which is shocking. So, how is it that in a world where there are now more marketing coaches, business coaches, consultants and trainers than ever before, that more businesses are failing than ever? Surely with so much information and support at hand, failure would be impossible, right? Unfortunately, it's more inevitable than impossible, and that's because it comes down to the fuel (marketing) you are using and the vehicle (business model) you are putting it into. Let's explain that further...

Many of the businesses from around the world that have been through our 12-week B.R.A.N.D. Accelerator Programme have usually already spent thousands on marketing consultants or business coaches before they found out about us. Employees who are starting a business for the first time invest their life savings into it, only to find they focused on fuel and not the vehicle. It breaks our hearts to find that they've invested thousands in time and money trying to get the help they needed to move them forward, but hardly any of it worked. We find out that they wasted months and even years of their own time trying to do it themselves. And then when they eventually did pay a consultant or coach to pour some more fuel in to help it move forward, it moved in inches rather than miles. They learned more confusing "stuff" online and tried that. They bought tickets to marketing and business growth courses and learned more "fuel," but that still didn't get the result they were looking for. It's disappointing to say the least. So, what was wrong with this strategy all along and how can you learn from their mistakes?

We will tell you now as we tell them: it makes no difference whatsoever how many courses you take, how many books you read or how many back stage passes you can get to free content. All of this is fuel that you keep pouring into a vehicle that has a broken steering wheel. You have to look at the vehicle first! If the Sat-Nav isn't programmed for the right destination, the steering wheel is locked in the wrong direction, three of the wheels are flat and there's a flipping great hole in the fuel tank, the only place your vehicle is going to drive you is up the wall!

All joking aside, you can have the best product or service in the world. But if the right research wasn't done before launching the business, then no meaningful destination can be programmed in. Without a destination, the business model won't be right and the plan (if there even is a plan) cannot support it. Therefore, no amount of coaching, mentoring or marketing will ever drive you anywhere, because all the fuel you put into it will just be evaporating out the other end, wasted.

However, with the right research, a solid business model, a well thought out strategy and plan, a customer journey, products and services you know will work (because you are now creating them based on customer demand and proof), all the marketing you do will be far more effective and efficient in generating results. As a personal brand, this should be your priority, as you might not yet have a business brand behind you to back you up.
Seriously, if you want to build a personal brand that leads in your industry and stands out like a beacon of best practice, then you really need to do your research. Yes, it takes time that you probably feel you don't have. Yes, it's going to make your brain hurt. Yes, it's going to take you more time and energy to do something with the results of your research. But you will also be doing something that none of your competitors can be bothered to do and that's why YOU deserve to lead instead of them.

There are some fatal brand strategy mistakes you will make if you don't put the right things in place in the right order. It's best to get this part of your plan right before you have to undo what you've already done. Here's a free tool to help you do that: It's our Marketing Planning Wheel, which gives you 12 basic steps to follow, so you start putting the right things in place now to build your business: ***http://howtobuildabrand.org/ marketing-planning-wheel/***

| Let's move on to ASSOCIATION... |

Building **BELIEF** in your personal brand in step one, and doing your **RESEARCH** in step two is fundamental to the success of your personal and business brand strategy. However, knowing what to do with the results of that research once you have them is another thing entirely. This next vital step is about creating a strong personal attachment and association to your business, whenever your prospects see or hear a certain thing consistently. Whether you are there personally to communicate what you do, or you are communicating your message through your website and other people via word of mouth, this step will help your brand to start owning a piece of their minds. This is about:

- **Attracting** your ideal customers by truly understanding their needs
- **Uncovering** the hidden areas of potential in your business
- **Building** better quality relationships with your ideal customers
- **Knowing** EXACTLY what to market to them, when, and how
- **Creating** a plan so you know where to find them and what to say when you do!
- **Having** a clear and memorable benefits-driven pitch that hooks them in
- **Creating** a solid customer service strategy
- **Making** all the marketing you ever do in future more productive and profitable

One of the eight activities we do in the "Advanced Customer Profiler" stage of the B.R.A.N.D. Accelerator programme is to get very clear about who your ideal customer really is. Even if you aim the most fantastic product or service in the world at someone who doesn't have a need or desire for it at the time you are promoting it, you are going to completely miss the point. If your ideal customer doesn't feel that what you deliver is aimed directly at them when they are experiencing the pain you know how to solve, you have quite possibly just lost them forever. Worse still, you might lose them to one of your competitors, who actually profiled them, listened to their needs and gave them what they wanted when they needed it. It's critical that you acquire a PHD in your customer's problems and that's what you need to do during this next step!

At the very minimum, here are three things you need to do now:

1. Describe your ideal customers in detail (get very, very, VERY detailed!)
2. Locate where they are hanging out in the highest concentration.
3. Listen to what they are saying and start helping them with whatever they need.

One of our key success strategies at How To Build A Brand is down to us being as helpful as possible in ways outside of what we make money doing. Sounds simple, eh? Yes, it really is that simple, but this means more than just being nice to people and paying lip service to your customer support once they start spending money with you. This is about your personal brand caring for people who aren't even your customers yet, as if they were your best friends. You need to start building your personal credibility in the strongest way possible by positioning yourself as the key to all your customer's problems – not just their recruitment problem. This is something we do extremely well and it has enabled us to build our brand into places we could never have got into just on our own merit.

Here's an example... Sonia was at a networking event that we also happened to attend. We met and introduced ourselves to each other and she asked what we do. Instead of going head long into our business, our immediate response was to turn the attention back to Sonia and get her to talk about her business. As she was talking, we asked intelligent questions about the challenges of her industry and who would be an ideal customer for her. What pains was her business experiencing and what kind of support did she think would be the best course of action for her? Everything Sonia said gave us more information to help her move forward.

Our aim was to introduce Sonia to at least three people who would either be an ideal customer for her, a great strategic partner to refer business to her or give her one of the tools we had created to help her move forward. We didn't talk about her branding once.

What happened? Well, as a result of being so helpful and introducing her to the people who helped her move forward, we had placed ourselves as clearly well connected. Our personal brands were glowing in her eyes and Sonia positioned us in her mind as key people of influence. She started to come to us whenever she needed ANYTHING, including a chimney sweep (this genuinely did happen!) and we got her one. Then, when Sonia needed an overhaul of her brand identity and website, who did she come to first? Us. Not only that, but in the meantime, she had referred us to at least another six businesses who needed our help, because even though we didn't talk about ourselves, we knew she would do her research on us and what she would find would be consistent, trustworthy and credible.

Many brands fail because they target anyone and everyone without first backing themselves up with a strong personal identity everywhere they might be found. They then try to sell them something that doesn't fit.

Or they broadcast across all the social networks instead of watching, listening and responding in a helpful way with what they actually need. These are very dangerous and expensive strategies that don't just cost you money; they will cost you your reputation as well and in recruitment – this is crucial.

Now is the time to get very focused, because when you watch and listen carefully enough, your ideal customers will tell you absolutely everything you need to know, create, sell and up-serve.

| Let's now talk about NURTURING... |

Ahhh... this is our most favourite part of the personal brand building process! In our business, we have a role that is totally dedicated to the creation of WOW experiences. This is a permanent role that is purely there to serve in the greatest way that we can for our customers. Their job is to proactively contact customers to find out what they need, how our service could be improved, what they have seen our competitors doing that we should be doing too, what we are missing and how could we make them say WOW again. This keeps us at the forefront of our customers' minds and therefore at the forefront of our industry in their opinion – and it's their opinion that matters most when it is they who are going to recommend us to others!

| Who is going to be the leader of WOW experiences in your business? |

A WOW experience is something you give to your customers that they haven't paid for. It goes beyond what you have promised to deliver and gives them another tick in the bonding box. This not only keeps you continually in touch with your customers to ensure you are still the first company or recruiter on their minds when they need what you provide, but it also keeps them bonded and loyal to your brand, so whenever they are contacted by one of your competitors they don't just tell them to go away, they come and tell you about it! This is VERY powerful and will give you consistent feedback as to what they are doing to try to get ahead of you. It's the kind of market research that money cannot buy and it will continually place you at the forefront of your industry, as you will always know what's going on.

An example of WOW experiences is that we constantly give, give, and give to our prospects, before they even become a customer. It may be that they get free video tips through our social media channels, free downloads and tools via our website or free training via our online webinars. This is such a great opportunity to start getting them to connect you to your topic and create the beginnings of the bond. Then, when they take the next step to buy our book, or attend one of our monthly B.R.A.N.D. Building Bootcamps at **www.BrandBuildingBootcamp. co.uk**, they receive free training by video that helps them to get the most out of the experience they have bought into. They also then receive some other great WOWs and resources throughout the day, as well as free access to our growing global community of business owners leading up to the event.

Many of the things we do are not part of the sale. They are given before, during and after the sale to consistently build greater rapport.

So, what could you do? What are some of the things you could do to give your prospects and customers of the future a big WOW? If I were you, I'd be jumping straight on the phone to ask people you already know, so you go out and give them EXACTLY what they want. This certainly beats assuming and then missing the mark completely.

| Finally, let's talk about DOMINATION... |

It's a tough statement to make, but we stand by it 100%...

'If you aren't leading, you are losing'.

If you genuinely know that you are going to deliver a service that is second to none in your industry, then you deserve to be seen, heard and felt EVERYWHERE. Don't worry if your competitors are already hanging around in those places. Just take the lead to put your brand in the number one position that sits in the minds and hearts of your ideal customers. With a solid strategy, you'll go out and claim your place in the marketplace in a way that is so strong that they will never be able to catch up with you.

To achieve this kind of domination, however, your personal brand must be visible in all the places that your ideal customers are spending their time and money. You also need to focus on building relationships with other non-competing business owners who share the same target customers as you. This will lead to referral opportunities in great abundance, especially once trust is established and they have a large list to introduce you to. But this all needs to be part of a greater plan.

Don't fall into the trap that so many other recruiters fall into, where they pay little, random or no attention to this part of their business growth plan. You can't complain that you are achieving feast and famine results with poor cash flow, if you are applying a feast and famine visibility strategy with no investment. To achieve consistent results and rewards, you need a consistent and rewards focused brand communications plan. Yes, it's going to cost you some time and money to do this. Yes, you are going to feel like you are going backward to go forward. However, just as you would invest in making sure the foundations of a property were safe and strong before you built on it, building the foundation of your brand will be the best investment you ever make in your business. Your brand is what your entire business as a recruitment specialist is going to be built on and you cannot expect your customers to invest in you if you aren't prepared to invest in yourself first.

Here's a piece of serious advice for you though when looking for a brand strategy company… Don't cut corners. If you think it costs a lot to hire a professional, just wait and see what it costs you to hire an amateur! Your reputation is at stake here and, as we said earlier, a lot of business owners come to us with businesses that are broke and broken from taking short cuts and we can't help them. This is your opportunity to do the right things in the right order, so you get it right first time around.

| What should a Brand Communications Strategy include? |

At its most basic level, a successful Brand Communications Strategy should achieve a massive amount of positive exposure for your business, using focused key messages about your brand in a way that can be measured both online and offline. It should look like the Marketing Planning Wheel we gave you in Step 2. Download it here if you haven't already done so: ***http://howtobuildabrand.org/marketing-planning-wheel/***

This 12-week planning wheel is exactly what we used to launch How To Build A Brand. It has proven itself time and again, not only on thousands of our customers' businesses around the world, but also on six of our own businesses prior to the sale of our last business in 2013. The results speak for themselves every time.

When How To Build, A Brand launched in January 2014, our company went from zero list of contacts (we'd sold all our contacts with the last business, so it meant starting from scratch again) and zero income, to £18,000 per month in retainer cash flow. The financial result spoke volumes, yet that wasn't the only positive result! This strategy also took our brand name, "How To Build A Brand" from 473,000,000 in the Google search engine results to #3 on the first page of Google. All of this happened in just 12 weeks following the skeleton of this plan! We even had competitors contacting us from all over the world to find out how we had achieved domination in such a short space of time! All this did was prove to us yet still that we are the world leading #1 brand for creating world leading personal and business brand strategies. Even our competitors don't know how to do what we achieved and if they can't achieve it for themselves, they definitely can't do it for their customers!

So, if you want to attract a thriving list of happy customers who value you, pay you more than anyone else in your industry and give you the freedom to spend more time doing what you love, then follow our model.

And if you need any help adding the flesh and muscle to it, get in touch at *www.howtobuildabrand.org*, so we can help you to build the strong recruitment brand that deserves to be seen, heard and felt in the world when you are ready to launch.

Contact Sammy and Miles personally to ask them your questions on Twitter at:*@SammyBlindell @MilesFryer*

NEXT STEPS...

| Next Steps... |

Congratulations! You have completed **Recruitment Gems Uncovered** and, by using any one of the techniques I've shared with you in this book consistently, you will change your results.

By investing your time in reading this book, you are already ahead of many in your industry. The truth is, your own personal development never stops.

If you think you're already the best and the finished article, trust me, just thinking that way proves you're not. The true trait of a successful individual is a consistent thirst for knowledge, wanting to know more, learn more, improve, and having an open mind to receive. That's the sign of someone who thrives for success. That's a sign of YOU.

You've made a promising and powerful start! If you're like me, you won't want to stop there so here are some ways you can continue your growth:

 Recruiters' Academy TV

This channel is perfect for anyone in the recruitment industry; by subscribing you'll be exposed to regular updates on the industry, learn new techniques or simply be refreshed and reminded of key recruitment modules that can help you stay on track. If you're a manager or recruitment business owner, Recruiters' Academy TV will bring you updates on the market, training tips you can use with your team as well as interviews with experts from the industry that could help make a difference in your agency/ business.

Just go to: ***https://www.youtube.com/channel/ UCmzLYTMiVX2PA0X0GINIbLw?view_as=public***

If you have any challenges, questions or topics you would like more information on, then email me at: ***Deenita@viamii.com*** and I'll make sure I answer them through Recruiters' Academy TV.

You can also connect with me via the following platforms:

https://uk.linkedin.com/in/deenitapattni

www.facebook.com/talentatviamii

@deenitaP

www.viamii.com/training

In closing, I want to say thank you for taking time to read this book and trusting me with your career. More importantly, thank you for trusting YOU and believing that the advice, guidance and knowledge shared in this book will work and help you reach your goals to become the best recruiter you can be for your clients, candidates, colleagues and for the industry. The Recruitment Industry needs people who are passionate about the industry and want to be part of it long-term in a way that serves all concerned for the better.

I believe that training is an imperative ingredient in nurturing talent within the recruitment industry and although you can learn a lot from books, videos, blogs and social media, there is no substitute for live, interactive training.

If you'd like the opportunity to meet me face-to-face and experience my training first-hand, then get in contact by emailing me at Deenita@viamii. com for a free consultation. I'll be happy to spend time with you and find out about your business and specific training needs to create a bespoke training programme for you.

Finally, as a fellow recruitment professional, I would love to hear your comments, feedback and testimonials on this book. Please feel free to email them to me with a picture of you holding my book.

Together, we'll be

'PIECING TOGETHER FUTURES'

| About the Author |

Deenita Pattni is an international Trainer, Mentor, Speaker, Author and Professional Speaking Coach. She is the founder of The Mind Vehicle Ltd & Viamii, a training and development company helping individuals live and recognise the true potential inside them. Her flagship training programmes include: **The Rapid Recruitment Engine™**, a full-service training programme that equips recruitment professionals with the skills they need to succeed in the industry, and **Linked In – Cash In Converter™**, an implementation workshop that trains entrepreneurs and recruitment professional on how to leverage LinkedIn to benefit their business, and **ACE Coach & Mentor Accreditation Accelerator™**, a 2-day programme that helps senior managers and leaders empower and motivate teams. She is also the Head Coach, Mentor & Professional Speaker & Speaking Coach for Andy Harrington's Jet Set Speaker brand, teaching entrepreneurs worldwide how to speak and share their message from stage and as the Head of Operations for Jet Set Speaker Limited consults and contributes to the success of this global business.

Born and bred in the heart of London, she grew up in a working-class family and was raised by her parents to achieve success and dreams in whatever she believed possible. Influenced by her father, who had an inner entrepreneurial flair overlooked by the need to raise an extended family, Deenita worked in the corporate world for almost 17 years before allowing her entrepreneurial spirit to come to the forefront. A big advocate of personal development, Deenita took time out of her daily routine to attend seminars and workshops that changed her beliefs and perspectives on what success meant and how she could achieve it.

Today, she speaks on stages around the world including Europe, Australia, South Africa, Singapore to name a few, sharing her knowledge and knowhow with others. Her big WHY is to help professionals overcome their limiting beliefs and feel empowered and encouraged to reach the business success they dream of by ongoing investment and development in themselves.

Printed in Great Britain
by Amazon